LOser GOes First

LOser GOes First

My Thirty-Something Years of Dumb Luck and Minor Humiliation

Dan Kennedy

 THREE RIVERS PRESS • NEW YORK

Published by Three Rivers Press, New York, New York.
Member of the Crown Publishing Group, a division of Random House, Inc.
www.crownpublishing.com

Three Rivers Press and the Tugboat design are
registered trademarks of Random House, Inc.

Originally published in hardcover by Crown Publishers,
a division of Random House, Inc., New York, in 2003.

Portions of this work appeared previously on
McSweeneys.net and Pindeldyboz.com.

Portions of this work were taken from the author's
previous performances at Stories at The Moth.

Printed in the United States of America

Design by Barbara Sturman

Library of Congress Cataloging-in-Publication Data

Kennedy, Dan
    Loser goes first : my thirty-something years of
dumb luck and minor humiliation / Dan Kennedy.
        p. cm.
    1. American wit and humor.   I. Title.
    PN6165.K46   2003
    818'.602—dc21   2003002440

ISBN 1-4000-5374-9

10 9 8 7 6 5 4 3 2 1

First Paperback Edition

In Memory of Milton E. Haynes

CONTENTS

LOser GOes First

1

AllRight, California!
Are You Ready to Rock!

(I'm Not)

Christmas Eve 1978, and I'm ten years old. The August of one's life, really, if you're anything like me. I can remember staring at our white suburban ceiling and being keenly aware that the good days wouldn't last forever now that I was sliding down the slippery dark slope of double-digit numbers. I fell asleep wanting one thing: a black Gibson Les Paul guitar like the one Peter Frampton played. And like the one Pete Townshend from the Who played. And Ace Frehley from Kiss. The guitar would be my passport into the coolest band in our neighborhood. The *only* band in our neighborhood . . . Jokerz. It was Tim

Caldwell's band and they were going to play the next Valentine's Day dance at school: the gig that would change everything for me. The gig that would make me no longer a quiet loner who never spoke up or took what he wanted in this life. Every girl in sixth grade would be there, plus the high-school girls who had to "volunteer" to do things like serve punch or take tickets at the door as part of their detention. They were there usually because they were caught smoking or fighting and made to perform this sort of community service as part of their punishment. And my gorgeous, sort of Dyan Cannonish homeroom teacher, Mrs. Davis, would be there. And they would all be in front of the stage. And I would be on the stage, the new guitarist in Tim's band.

When I woke up on Christmas morning, I walked down the hallway and approached the family Christmas tree in what felt like the first truly religious Christmas celebration ever held in our suburban Southern California household. I walked with the epic pace of a bishop . . . with the timing of a monk and a casual sort of confidence not unlike that of a pope or a church owner/manager or whatever men happened to walk in churches with a deliberate pace. I don't know that much about churches. I knelt before the presents under the tree like I imagine the men I was just mentioning might kneel in ceremony. My parents always went the extra mile. They worked hard, putting in extra hours at their jobs, and they'd given my sister, Trish, and me more than we thought we'd ever get. I opened my presents.

- Maroon velour pullover shirt with a tan stripe on the chest

- Blank journal with photo of autumn leaves and covered bridge on front
- Special kind of calculator that easily figured interest and appreciation on real-estate investments (?)

I was confused by the calculator, and I thought I might have even accidentally opened a present meant for my father. I looked over at him and figured the big smile on his face meant one of two things:

- That he was also confused and trying to figure out why I got the "Loan Arranger" calculator he wanted, or . . .
- His smile was some sort of vote of confidence in a bright future that he assumed awaited me in real estate.

There were other presents. But none of them was a black Gibson Les Paul guitar. But then my parents said there was one more present. They loved to do this. God bless them for this, I thought, a little surprised that the whole religious feeling was still with me in our little ceremony. My parents would let us get real happy about the other stuff and say thank you and everything, and then my dad would look over at my mom and in his best relaxed-guy, confident, comic timing say, "Honey, I think we just might have forgotten one or two things." And that was our cue to really turn up the excitement. So you would always want to kind of keep your excitement to a certain level so you had a little extra to lay on when the final round came. Sort of play at level seven so you could go up to ten for the final gift encore. Maybe this year my final present would be the black Les Paul guitar.

So my parents came back into the living room. With that we were told to close our eyes, and we did. We could hear them getting our final present in position in front of each of us. I strained my ears to hear the sound of an open E note in case my father's blue terry-cloth bathrobe had accidentally brushed against the strings of my new black Les Paul guitar.

Nothing.

Perfectly silent.

And in that silence came a moment of panic and this thought raced through my head: I'm a really quiet kid. What if I only secretly and quietly pined for my guitar? What if they had no idea I wanted it? I wonder if I ever even said I wanted it out loud. Like right now, for instance. I'm only thinking all of this, but I might remember it as something I said out loud.

I closed my eyes even tighter in hopes of somehow hearing better. I saw myself taking my new black Gibson Les Paul to the gig. The gig goes great. The Nieblas Middle School Valentine's dance has never been rocked like this before. And in the middle of playing "Surrender" by Cheap Trick, Karen McCall (hot) throws a note up onstage. I can't stop to read it, because I'm in the middle of a big solo that is making everyone in our school hold their hands up in the air and sway them back and forth. So I motion to Bruce, our roadie, to get the note and tell me what it says. He holds it up in front of me while I play. It says "Will you be mine?" and then it has a check box that says "yes" and another check box that says "no." I yell above my solo to tell Bruce to mark the box that says "yes." I'm, like, kind of yelling in his ear while I keep playing the solo, "Dude . . . check 'yes' and hand it back to her." He does it in a very uncaring way, as if he's done it a million times before. I don't mind his nonchalant attitude. He's not paid to worry about my love notes. He's paid to worry about our gear. When we come offstage into the multipurpose room, she's waiting for me in our dressing room (PE equipment closet), and since she is there it means we are together now. And there are other gigs like this one . . . and then middle school was over. And then there was high school. And we decided that it was time to grow up, because there were certain things that just didn't make sense now that we were young adults in the real world of high school.

So we dropped the z and become Joker. And we played everywhere, the coolest band at Fountain Valley High. And people loved us even more. And then we made the best move of our career: We dropped out of high school, because touring and making records was all we ever wanted to do and everything else was just getting in our way. Joker was finally on the radio and education would have to take a backseat to touring the States and Europe. We didn't need no education. We didn't need no thought control. No dock sarcasm? No ducks in chasm? I can never hear what they're saying in half of the Pink Floyd lyrics. The more we toured, the bigger things got. Karen couldn't take the pressure of having me away all of the time, so we broke up. But I don't mind . . .

It's all so fine /
'Cause I traded love to see the world /
See the world /
See the world

That's a lyric from one of our songs. Tim wrote it. It was called "Traded Love" and then in parentheses it said "See the World." And then the world all started to look the same to me. Because there was never time to actually see anything. When people ask me what it's like to see the world, I like to say, "Take a trip to your local airport five times in one day." Or sometimes I say, "It looks like the stadium in any city you've ever been in." Sometimes I'll combine those two and say, "Go to your local airport and hang out there for an hour or so, then drive to the nearest stadium and hang out there for the rest of day."

And then lawyers got involved. Seems there was a problem with being fifteen and not attending school, and so it was mandated that we have tutors on the road. My tutor was named Candy Sinsation. She was five feet nine, blond, wore fishnet stockings and leather boots, had long legs, and she had a flair for U.S. history and math. She taught me a lot, but she couldn't teach me to get over Karen. And she couldn't teach me to want any of this anymore, because I was already tired of being at the top. You know, there's a reason they call being on top of the charts being number one with a bullet. Because sooner / or later / you wanna shoot / all of this down. Also one of our songs. Tim could write 'em; I have to say that even to this day. I tried to bring a song in here and there, but usually my chords were cliché and the arrangements were strained.

The lyrics were usually esoteric fantasies too personal for people to relate to.

FOR KAREN

Music by Caldwell/Kennedy, Lyrics D. Kennedy
Published by Joker's Muse (ASCAP)

I have taken you here /
To the finest steak house in Orange County, California
And you look beautiful tonight /
Next to the unique plants /
And contemporary chrome lights.

And being here /
Means we're going together now. (Repeat x3)

Later, we are relaxing on /
An expensive modern art type of sofa /
And I let you know /
That this is my own apartment.

(Backup vocals: Somehow we both know that . . .)
Chorus:

Being here /
Means we're together now. (Repeat x3)

(Solo)

I have a Porsche Targa with a radar detector /
My parents don't live here /
I'm rich and legally /
Living away from them now /
It's called minor emancipation.

Yes, I still love them /
Karen, please be an adult about it /

I'll get you a daiquiri from /
The two-thousand-eight-hundred-dollar /
Professional machine in my kitchen /
Maybe tomorrow, we'll take a classy trip on /
A thirty-one-foot sailboat.

Daiquiris and talking /
Means we're together now. (Repeat x3)

I had spent my whole life (since I was eleven) trying to get to the top. Over two years and eight months of doing whatever it took to get there, and now that I was finally there, all I wanted to do was come down. Our plane took off from Wyoming, or China, or whatever one rainy morning, and I closed my eyes and wished to God for all of this to stop. I closed my eyes so tight and wished so hard. The jet engine's whine turned into the voices of my parents.

They were saying, "Hey, guy . . . you can open your eyes now." And I did.

I'm still in the living room Christmas morning and my sister is ecstatic, laughing, smiling and thanking and hugging and jumping. She's looking at her final present, the cool leather handbag that she told our parents she wanted. To this day my sister is really good at getting what she wants. Great career. Great husband. Great house.

And I was staring at my final present: a silver-and-black General Electric portable cassette player.

My dad leans over and goes, "You've never come right out and said it, but it's kind of clear to your mom and me that you seem to like music."

I'm staring. I shouldn't be staring. He tries to break my eye contact by talking.

"And this plays music!"

"Well, it records it, honey," Mom clarified. "He can record songs from the radio with it."

I spent the rest of my Christmas break in my maroon velour pullover, using my new calculator to figure out the interest on housing loans and the projected appreciative value of various houses on our block . . . and trying to figure out how the hell I would join Tim Caldwell's band with a General Electric portable cassette player. When I wasn't trying to figure fake real-estate deals, I was writing in my blank journal—with the covered bridge and autumn leaves on the cover—about how nothing was working out for me. At first I didn't really even know what the covered bridge was. We've lived in Orange County, California, since I was born, so I don't think I've ever seen one. I thought it was an elevated cabin or garage of some kind. Wait, there's one of these on the front of the margarine my mom buys at Albertsons. And also on the wheat crackers she likes.

On my first day back at school after the Christmas break, I heard the rumor that Tim had gotten in trouble and was going to get suspended. Part of his sentence was that Jokerz wouldn't be playing the Valentine's dance. Or any dance. So now, in my darkest hour, it seemed nothing much mattered. Even if I did figure out a way to join the band, there would be no gig—and so really, what was the point? There was a band called Magik that had played a lunchtime assembly last year before summer break, but nobody liked them, so they probably wouldn't get the

Valentine's gig. Plus, they were all in their forties and they probably didn't need a ten-year-old guitarist.

I had an idea: I would approach the principal and the president of the student body about letting me be the deejay for the dance.

"I understand you guys are in a little bit of a bind with the Valentine's dance as far as entertainment goes."

I explained to them that they were in luck, and that I had gotten some "General Electric deejay equipment" for Christmas. It was official. I would deejay the dance. They would supply a turntable and PA system, to fill out my setup.

So on the afternoon of the dance, I showed up early and set up my "system." That night, a friend of mine named Mike helped me out. He would cue up records while I cued up songs on the cassette player. He would go talk to people out on the dance floor and take requests. The gig was going really well . . . until my little tape player broke for some reason. I was stuck with only the turntable, which was right at the end of Led Zeppelin's "Stairway to Heaven." In a panic, with no other music to segue to, I just started "Stairway to Heaven" again from the beginning, figuring it would buy me some time (eight minutes and two seconds) to figure out how to fix the damn cassette player so I could play the next song. But I couldn't fix the stupid thing. I couldn't make heads or tails of how it was put together inside.

I ended up playing "Stairway to Heaven" three and a half times in a row.

At the beginning of the third time, it was clear that everybody hated me and that this was the worst dance in the world. The girls were all laughing at me because they could see I was freaking out. The daring couples of the most popular and confident people in my school were stranded on the floor and slowly rotating in that teenage slow-dance rotisserie daze. Each time the guys' faces came around in the slow rotation, they would lean over the girls' shoulders and tell me that they were going to kick my ass after the dance for making them slow-dance to "Stairway to Heaven" for well over twenty minutes straight.

Playlist For Nieblas Middle School Valentine's Dance
"Hello There" (Cheap Trick)
"Whip It" (Devo)
"Runnin' with the Devil" (Van Halen)
"London Calling" (the Clash)
"Start!" (the Jam)
"Turning Japanese" (the Vapors)
"Stairway to Heaven" (Led Zeppelin)
"Stairway to Heaven" (Led Zeppelin)
"Stairway to Heaven" (Led Zeppelin)
One half of "Stairway to Heaven"
(Led Zeppelin)

This was not what I had planned for my life. I was going to be a rock star, but I didn't get the right kind of guitar from my parents. That's when I learned that being a rock star has nothing to do with depending on your parents to buy you the right guitar. And it's not about just closing your eyes and being swept away on a world tour filled with women and private jets, and spending a typical day having your breakfast in North Dakota and then dinner in Japan or Indonesia. No, it comes down to rehearsing, writing and rewriting, playing gigs where you load your own equipment in and out, and sleeping on floors and couches until you can afford motels; it comes down to doing the work.

And when I finally realized this, uh . . . I quit. I mean, you know, I don't need that, man. Why do I want to rehearse in some guy's parents' garage on a Tuesday afternoon when I know that no girls will even be there? I needed to pull all of my energy into trying to be *less* of a misfit and loner at this point. In the back of my mind, I don't think I was so serious about quitting. I mean, rock stars did this all the time. They said they were breaking up or retiring, and then, sooner or later, they were back onstage. A friend of mine told me that Pete Townsend once went over eight years without playing guitar and that Townsend felt it made him a better player. Clearly the first thing I had to do to be a rock star was not play guitar for eight to ten years.

TAKING A 70'S SUPERMODEL TO MEET THE PARENTS

Following is a transcript of a conversation I overheard my friend Mike having with his mother in 1978 after returning home from the Nieblas Middle School Book Fair. I just kind of stood off to the side acting like I wasn't there when she started freaking out.

HIS MOM: Did you get something you like?
MIKE: Yeah.

HIS MOM: We have to get all of your work done after school on Friday so we can leave early Saturday morning.

MIKE: Okay.

HIS MOM: What is that?

MIKE: What?

HIS MOM: That. In your hand.

MIKE: A poster.

HIS MOM: A poster? Where did you get that?

MIKE: I bought it at the book fair.

[Mike unrolls poster of Cheryl Tiegs standing in bathing suit against blue background.]

HIS MOM: You spent the money on a poster?!

MIKE:

HIS MOM: What are you going to read on the drive? You were supposed to get a book! You know that!

MIKE:

ME:

HIS MOM:

MIKE: You said I could get whatever. . . .

HIS MOM: Whatever *book* you wanted!

MIKE: God, what's the—

HIS MOM: What the hell do you plan on doing for three hours on the way to Grandma and Grandpa's house? You're just going to stare at this woman for three hours in the back of the car? Goddamn it, Michael, I hope you enjoy looking at her!

MIKE: I do. God.

MY FANTASY SCHOOL NEWSPAPER ARTICLE:
TEACHER AND STUDENT LEARN LESSONS
OF LOVE

What do you do when you really like your homeroom teacher? Well, you could write the school administration a glowing letter, you could bring her an apple, or you can get a nice five-room duplex apartment with her in one of Southern California's most exclusive seaside communities. And that's just what sixth-grade student Dan Kennedy did when he realized his crush on his Cannonesque homeroom teacher, Mrs. Davis, was more than just a crush. "People are making a really big deal about the twenty-year age thing, which has been getting a little old." The two of them start laughing at Kennedy's nimble and playful ability to always find a twist on words. It's eleven-thirty in the morning on a Saturday and we're having brunch on the deck of their Laguna Beach home. They seem happy. The deck is an odd mix of macramé plant holders, small statues of Buddha and other Zen paraphernalia, and a couple of Les Paul guitars that Kennedy is putting new strings on. When pressed a little further, Kennedy is quick to admit that the age thing can be a problem. "Who's Dick Cavett? She will mention him occasionally on the phone with a college friend, and I'll be lost." And what about the rare but inevitable lovers' quarrel? "Oh, God . . . I'm just lost when she's mad at me. I'm actually writing a song about how lost I am when she is mad at me. I have no idea what she's saying. One time she told me to 'ditch my Eisenhower administration mentality,' and I'm just standing there trying to figure out what to say back to her. One time I yelled something back about the Emancipation Proclamation, but I don't think it made much sense." According to neighbors, the controversial couple has more good days than bad. "Oh, you'll see them out at some of the restaurants around the community. Always laughing. Very romantic, if you can get past the age difference . . . Everyone says he's way beyond his peers when it comes to maturity," said neighbor Ron Helstrom. Saying that Kennedy is ahead of his sixth-grade peers is an understatement. In early September, when other boys were wallowing in the melancholy of silent crushes on Mrs. Davis and her perfect hair and golden California tanned skin, Kennedy did the unthinkable. "It was pretty clear to me early on that this was more than a crush, so I basically said, 'Look, I know about everything—periods, sex, bras—all of it. So let's get honest here and start talking about taking this to the true love level.' And she seemed to feel the same way." The two plan on keeping it business as usual at school. "Yeah, everything's exactly the same when we're in the classroom. The only difference is that afterward we are sophisticated adult lovers who make love in an expensive condominium." Regardless of how you feel about this student and teacher stepping up their love commitment, you have to admit they both seem to have a lot of class.

DETENTION RAP SHEETS:
MEET THE HIGH-SCHOOL DELINQUENTS WHO
"VOLUNTEER" AT OUR SIXTH-GRADE DANCE

Becky Reese (Ticket Taker)

Becky could staff sixth-grade dances for the remaining two years of her high-school career and still be in the hole with detention time. Claim to fame: showed up at ex-boyfriend's parents' house and set their car on fire in the driveway after beating it maniacally with the steel garden rake. Ex was smart enough to know that trying to stop her would've meant spending the rest of his life explaining eight parallel scars tracing a path from a glass eye to a numb upper lip.

Tammy Cox (Punch and Snacks)

We've heard every Cox/Cock/Cocks joke you can possibly spin, so save it. Plus, if she hears it, she'll kick your skinny sixth-grade ass. Claim to fame: on prom night last year, left dance early and snuck into the Andersons' back-yard with twenty-pound bag of lawn fertilizer she stole from new housing tract. Dumped entire bag into the Jacuzzi. Brad Anderson and his popular friends came back to have a pool party at his parents' house and found what was essentially a piping-hot vat of cow shit awaiting them.

Pam Tiller (Coat Check and Backpack Check)

When she was here at Nieblas she was the poster girl for clean, conservative, preppy living, spending summers sailing at Catalina Island with her picture-perfect family.

But then high school . . . and the drinking, the Mohawk, the leather, and the phrase "This Side Up" tattooed on her stomach. Claim to fame: kicking faculty out of announcer's booth at homecoming football game, locking herself in there, and then screaming phrases like "Eat the rich" and "I am the Walrus" and "The prom queen's got a gun!" over the stadium PA system at pleasant and confused parents and students in bleachers.

JOURNAL ENTRIES: PAST THE BRIDGE AND AUTUMN LEAVES ON THE COVER

- As far as I can figure, will take twenty-two years before the Kellers' payments affect principal of their home loan. Unless I'm using this thing wrong.

- **Song Idea:** Nothing going right is not wrong— she is ~~Even loving the wrong is loving someone~~ EVER loving the wrong.

- **Dream:** Mom and Dad and Trish and me on a tram going through parking lot of NBC Studios. Tour guide (jock who thinks he's a pro comedian or something) points out parking space reserved for Johnny Carson. Makes some lame joke about it that T laughs at regardless. Just then Carson pulls into the space in a tan Mercedes. Tram is going wild. Bows from side to side as fat tourists wave arms and crane necks to get a look. Carson could've probably made his way into work without a hassle if it wasn't for Sporto pointing out his parking space to a hundred and fifty

tourists on a tram. Johnny appears to be in a
good mood and actually steps over to the tram
to say hello. Asks me if jokes in monologue are
ready. Tell him yes, but that I'll be in around two-
thirty to tighten a few jokes up. My parents and
sister have this look in their eyes like somehow
I know that they knew all along that I am head
writer at the *Tonight* show. They admit there's no
way they can control me now. Even Mr. Popular
Jock Tour Guide is trying to kiss my ass by
complimenting show's writing into his microphone and very obviously within my earshot.

*[Drawing of a bad Gene Simmons. Tongue is
not long enough and eye makeup lopsided.]*

*[Graffiti in margin: KEZY-FM Kicks Back—
KEZY-AM Kicks Ass!]*

*[Picture of . . . what looks like bike wheel and
written next to it: Mongoose frame—Redline
cranks—alloy rims.]*

- Talking about moving lately. Almost every day.
  And it's this thing that I think we are going to get
  serious about. They kind of mentioned it to me
  yesterday officially.

  ?? Mom and Dad have friend that moved to
  mountains somewhere.

2

I Was a Teenage Bass Fisherman

Ah, look. There it is. The covered bridge. Just like the cover of my little blank journal, except now it's in larger scale. And real. Just outside the passenger window of our Oldsmobile Vista Cruiser station wagon.

My parents moved to a very small, rural Northern California town in 1980. In this town, there were a handful of things that I found different from our suburban life in Southern California, differences that were made clear to me in the somewhat blunt social setting of a rural eighth-grade classroom. For instance, my remarks or jokes containing a reference to the 1972 hit motion picture

Deliverance were generally frowned upon by classmates. At first I thought the rude remarks, threats, and tentative dates set for after-school fistfights that I received were the committed gestures of a bunch of impassioned young men defending what they misinterpreted as an attack of film director John Boorman's cinematic adaptation of the book penned by American poet James Dickey. But as it turned out, their remarks and threats were completely unrelated to their tastes in film and literature.

"Guys, I was just joking about *Deliverance* being filmed here."

"[Making their voices really high-pitched] Guys, I was just joking about *Deliverance* being filmed here."

"[Returning to a normal voice] Why're you wearing girls' pants?"

Should I have monitored how many of those "suburban family moves to the woods, befriends wildlife, and lives happily ever after" television shows and movies my parents might have been watching?

Maybe.

Okay, yes.

My yearbook nominations for best hair and best personality that I got in a strange fluke of chance just before moving from Southern California were worth exactly zero here. My somehow managing to kill time with the hottest girl at Nieblas Middle School meant zero in this town. The majority of my personal effects from my seventh-grade suburban Southern California life were *not* going over well here in this little mountain town. For instance, the Ocean Pacific shorts and T-shirts that I finally secured through massive lobbying to the parental units were routinely mistaken for, um, girls' clothing here. And the feathered haircut that I fought tooth and nail for, for two years straight, that I finally got my dad to allow me to ask the family barber for, was apparently considered more of a, uh, girl's haircut here. I don't know what my surfer necklace made out of Hawaiian pookah shells that I got from my sister's surfer boyfriend would have been considered, because I left it packed away in its box . . . but I think, you know, probably a girl's necklace. So there I was, and everything I had worked to build was gone. I was finished. But what I didn't know then was that if I could make it through to summer, I would see a magazine cover that would change the way I was looking at things. Still, how did I get here?

Seems like the last thing I remember was going to sleep in my Southern California bedroom. My model boat that was actually a little transistor radio (power and volume was steering wheel, mast was antenna) was hidden next to my pillow and turned down low enough that my parents wouldn't hear me listening to the stations in L.A. and Orange County that played local punk and New Wave bands after midnight. If all went as planned, I would secretly stay up late listening to the Plimsouls, Oingo Boingo, and X, and then wake up at around seven-thirty to have a breakfast of the chocolate-sweetened cereal that (again . . . years of lobbying) I had finally convinced my mother to buy. Then I would ride my skateboard to school and enjoy things finally starting to go well for me. But something happened. At around one-thirty in the morning, the 1190 KEZY deejay named Lovely Rita came on the air and I knew something was wrong because she was crying and she was playing only Beatles songs, and she said that she would continue playing only Beatles songs all night even if it meant losing her job. Every time she came back on the air between songs that night, things in New York had gotten worse. And after it got to be the worst it could get to be that night, I swung the little boat's tiny wheel hard and far to the port side to turn it off, and ever since that night, 1980 has felt like falling asleep to the DJ crying and Beatles songs and then waking up to find we were living in the mountains.

The mountains. Not camping. Living.

It was clear to me right away that I was going to have to start building all over again. I had no idea what to do about the clothes, and I had a ton of dead inventory in my closet. Maybe compromise? Maybe still wear the so-called girls' shirt, but wear it with tough-looking jeans like Wrangler? Maybe keep wearing the so-called girls' clothes, but smoke cigarettes to balance it out? This was all shaping up to be kind of a bad small-town version of Bowie's gender-bending glam phase, and my second or third day of the eighth grade, I found myself in a threatening situation. She was big and was tough and was broad-shouldered and muscular and firm and strong, but I thought I was doing pretty well. It was fifth-period lunch, and I was sitting alone, except for the lunchroom worker (counts as having someone at your table) who was taking a smoke break and talking to me about the limited health insurance benefits of working part time in the school kitchen.

"[Inhale] They don't consider me a school district

employee if I'm working in the goddamn cafeteria [exhale], so I only get half of the district health shit."

I felt for this guy. He was clearly in a bind for insurance coverage, and to make matters worse, he was a pretty heavy smoker. But I didn't have the luxury of time to worry about other people's ships sinking; I was going down just as fast. I had finished my lunch and was sitting there eating a piece of beef jerky and listening to this school district lunch guy's insurance problems when she came up to me. She stood right in front of me, and she had a semicircle of friends watching this whole thing go down. And I'm looking at her and thinking that this girl has probably had a crush on me since the day I got here if she's got all her friends standing around her like this. I mean, why else would she bring all of these *guys* with her? I mean, it seems like one of them would be her boyfriend. (Think. Think, dammit. What are you going to say if she asks you to be her boyfriend? She's not altogether bad looking—in a rugged, outdoorsy, broad-shouldered, disheveled, flannel-shirt sort of way—but not exactly girl-friend material. I can lie and say I already have a girl-friend, but that can end up hurting her feelings in the long run. Just be honest and be thankful that somebody has feelings for you.) She would just have to accept that, and if it's not what she wanted to hear, she should've thought of that before she asked all of her friends to come along with her.

"Give me that beef jerky, Dick."

(Dick?)

"No."

And we both stood there, me with a playful grin, since I thought we were flirting, and her looking angry, and somehow shocked or in disbelief. And all her friends looked on with the same disbelief. Stillness. Neither of us budging an inch on our position. Oh my God, was she thinking I was going to kiss her? And then she stepped closer to me, like she had something to tell me that only I would get. Something that she has been waiting for a long time to say to somebody who would finally hear it and understand.

She said, "I should kick your ass. You're lucky I'm on probation."

There I was, a young man stuck in this mountain town, watching his personal stock plummet fast and hard in a daily downward spiral about as drastic as the decline in popularity that the Betamax and laser-disc movie-rental formats would suffer in the later part of the decade. I finished eighth grade struggling to adjust to life in the mountain town, then spent the summer keeping mostly to myself and hatching a plan to survive my fall enrollment in high school. I was spending all of my free time fishing, and that's when I saw the August issue of *Western Bass Fisherman Monthly*. On the cover was a man, probably in his late thirties or early forties. He was a winner. A champion. He had a sun-bleached feathered haircut. He was wearing Ocean Pacific shorts. He was holding an eight-pound largemouth bass in one hand, and a huge three-foot-by-six-foot check for fifty thousand dollars in the other. This was my time. I could do this. I had fished since

I was old enough to stand up in a boat with my father in Southern California.

Magazines were subscribed to, equipment catalogs were ordered, and I even started killing time sketching pictures of lures and naming them so that when my big break came, I would have an entrepreneurial venture ready to provide an income beyond my tournament winnings. Within weeks of starting the ninth grade, my school folders held mostly unfinished homework assignments and make-up exams, as well as notes on victory speeches/bass-fishing award acceptance speeches, and they were covered with the logos of my favorite boat manufacturers, which I tended to draw absentmindedly while daydreaming of big-money victories that would take me far from the classroom I was stuck sitting in. Inside the folders were rough sketches of the lures I was developing in my spare time. There was, for instance, the Silver Meanie™, which I would design and someday manufacture to imitate the spastic swimming patterns of a struggling injured minnow. The inside of my locker was plastered with pictures of bass-fishing pros like Roland Martin and Dee Thomas holding their winning catches at various championship tournaments. I had even recruited a couple of fellow freshmen into my little club. But there was still a fair share of tense and uneven exchanges with the sophomores, juniors, and seniors, even though I had traded my Southern California clothes for more basic jeans and various T-shirts, as well as hats and jackets that carried the logos of my favorite bass-fishing gear.

One day, me and my two fellow aspiring pro-fishermen

buddies were hanging out together at lunch, away from the others, gossiping about which fishing pros were using what lures to win tournaments at various lakes in North America, when we were interrupted by some seniors.

"What are you pretty little freshman girls doing eating your little lunches way down here?"

A quick study of the habitat of these guys, and the marks they made on their environment, revealed mostly drawings of pot leaves, beer logos, and animated men with large genitals. The animated men were always pictured approaching animated women who had speech bubbles above their heads that contained phrases like "I wanna suck it." These guys were cool . . . and . . . these guys had cars. Really cool cars.

"I just asked you a question, you little lame asses."

"Your cars kick ass, dudes. Killer stereos, too. Nice job." This offered to the seniors from my fishing buddy Bill.

Long pause.

(*Note:* Bill had recently read an article in *Bassmasters Magazine* that explained a simple trick that crayfish will sometimes use to thwart being attacked by large-mouth bass. If a bass approaches a crayfish aggressively on the lake bottom, they will raise their claws toward the fish in a very social manner, pinchers closed, and counter with what appears to be a sort of gentle pat on the fish's chest. The fish will pause, confused by what appears to be an almost social interaction, and further confused by two additional points of contact to focus on. Forgetful of its original intentions, the fish will swim away about half of the time.)

"Yeah," I added.

Pause continues.

"That's right . . . little . . . freshman . . . dicks," one of them said.

Confused by what appeared to be a social gesture, they moved on toward the parking lot, where they would most likely unwind by listening to their car stereos and blow off steam by spray-painting the phrase "AC/DC Kicks Ass" on the asphalt to reserve the parking spot they preferred for the semester. I dreamed of tournament victories and having to spray-paint "AC/DC Kicks Ass" in *two* parking spaces: one for my truck and one for my boat.

But I wouldn't be able to drive until my junior year, and I was only a freshman, so my acts of rebellion were still limited to defacing school-issued book covers with sketches of my Silver Meanie prototype lure as well as my other prototypes of various crawdad (Mister Pincherz™), frog (Green Meanie™), and worm (never got around to naming) imitations. There were also the clever lines that would be used to advertise my lures. I was responsible for felt-tip-pen graffiti gems like "The Green Meanie™ catches fish . . . not fishermen." I had finally achieved the prerequisite low grades of the rock star I had given up trying to be back in the sixth and seventh grades in Southern California. The only class I was doing even halfway decent in (C+) was my third-period art class, where I was spending the better part of the semester completing a detailed watercolor rendering of two northern-strain largemouth bass exhibiting some pretty typical cold-water behavior by lying dormant for the winter near a cluster of rocks and a submerged tree stump. My painting was actually a grid reproduction of the cover of the November issue of *Western Bass Magazine*, which featured a, well, painting of the same two fish doing the same thing. So my painting was a beautiful painting of a painting.

I had decided that I would try to gain some part-time employment in the professional bass-fishing trade, to be able to keep busy, make some money, and be closer to the business of bass fishing. I ended up getting a job at a local distributor of name-brand plastic worms and spinner baits that was located in a large corrugated aluminum garage in the industrial area of a neighboring town. My dad would give me a ride to my fishing-lure job after school every day. On Saturdays or holidays I would take the bus if there was work. Enter my new coworkers: Ricky (thirty-four), Steve (thirty), and Mary (age indeterminate in a very Keith Richards way).

We usually worked in pairs, and I got stuck with Ricky most of the time. He tied the skirts on half-ounce spinner baits while I counted the Fat Gitzits™ into piles of twenty-five. He made the most futile attempts at being funny. I heard Mary talking to him in the break-room one time, and he was saying that he was going to be trying some stand-up comedy at an open mic at this sports bar downtown. I was sorting out the Fat Gitzits™ and he looked at them and asked me if I "had any smoke." I handed him a bag of twenty-five smoke-gray-colored Fat Gitzits™ and he started laughing really hard, saying how they were "really gonna screw up his bong," and the more I didn't laugh, the harder he laughed, and with even more determination—like that hard-ass/stoner laugh where you think he's going to fight you if you don't start laughing—so

I faked a small laugh that you could tell was totally sarcastic. That was enough for him to tell everyone he was "making me crack up" while I was trying to count out my 25's.

Then there was a Saturday when I caught an early bus and made it in before anybody else. I liked the feeling it gave me when the others would file in at nine-thirty and my table was already lined out with 25's of Gitzits™ and Lil' Bits™ So I got in at seven-thirty, and nobody showed up until after ten. When Ricky and Steve came in, Ricky looked at my table and said, "What the hell are you, some kind of lawyer?" I had no idea why he would call me a lawyer just because I was so far ahead in my work already. So I kind of smiled (fake) and said, "Hey, what's up?" and he got this hard-ass look and said, "Now you're trying to get me to say something for the jury, huh? Sorry, Mr. Lawyer, no luck. You lose!" Ricky started laughing hard and Steve started laughing when he saw that Ricky thought this was funny. I just kept counting and then Mary came in and she stuck a Marlboro in her mouth. Crammed it in right next to the missing side tooth that made her look like the kind of witch you saw on a cheap Halloween decoration from one of the chain discount drugstores around there. She asked what was so funny, and Steve repeated the so-called joke *completely wrong*. He said, "Danny has been in here all morning working, and so when we came in, Ricky asked him if he needs a lawyer and then he goes, 'The jury says you lose, Judge!'" Mary started cracking up, and Steve was laughing even harder than the first time. Ricky looked like he was going to correct Steve for a minute, but then noticing that even a wrong version of the joke was a hit, he just kind of stood there and enjoyed the rewards of the poor joke revised to make it even worse. I just took out another big box of motor oil–color Lil' Bits (#LB 003) and split the box for counting. I shook my head hoping that I would seem kind of like a bad-ass who thought they were fools, but for some reason it made me feel like I was their aunt who thought they were "nutty kids" or something. I hated standing there feeling like a big, round, warmhearted woman counting four-inch plastic worms, and feeling like I was maybe even further away than ever from the success that would change everything for me.

On the bus home, some guy had a little transistor radio and it was playing that song by Rod Stewart called "Some Guys Have All the Luck," and I spent most of the ride trying to figure out if Rod Stewart meant that some *other* guys had all the luck (in which case I felt like a loser going home from my little fishing lure factory job, feeling like I had somehow managed to make my prospects even more limited), or if he was saying some guys *like him and me* had all the luck (in which case I felt like even if today was a little tough, I knew deep down inside that I was a lucky guy, and that somehow the universe would point me in the right direction).

When I got home, there was a note on my bedroom door that Bill had called. Turns out we could use his family's boat to fish an upcoming western bass night tournament on a nearby lake. My first tournament. What Rod Stewart obviously meant was that some guys like him and me had all the luck. This is the song I want them to play when they take my photo holding my first really large oversized check.

School days went by and work faded into the background as I prepared myself for the upcoming night tournament. We bought lights, but not just any lights—you need ultraviolet lights so that you can see but the fish can't see you. And we bought scores of lures that the fish could see better in the dark of night. We would be fishing on an enormous lake all through the night. Eventually the evening came when Bill's mom gave us a ride to the marina, backed the car and trailer down the launching ramp, and waited to let the boat slide from its trailer before wishing us luck and heading back home. There were maybe a hundred boats. And pros who were idols of mine. I had practiced my comments to the trade magazines a million times in my head and in the bathroom mirror. I had spent weeks of being chided by Ricky and Steve at work and hardly noticing, because I was rehearsing a victory speech in my head. And it had all led up to this moment. Well, not *this* moment. I mean, *this* moment wasn't anything that required a victory speech or comments to trade magazines. All we were doing was putting the boat in the water. *The* moment was still hundreds of moments away. But you know . . . this was still a pretty good moment.

VICTORY SPEECH IN CASE I WIN TOURNAMENT

Thank you. [Let applause continue.]

Thank you, everybody. [Still allow clapping.]

Thanks. [Make gesture with hand to indicate that they should let you speak now.]

I stand before you today, not just as a winner, not just as a great man, a great lure inventor, and a great overall U.S. citizen, but as an official champion.

[Let crowd cheer a little more.]

But I am not better than anybody. Well, let me re-phrase that: I am only better than the people whose names appear below mine on the board behind me, which lists the point standings. So, yes, I am better than the other fisher-men here today, but there are real champions out there who didn't even enter this tournament. Actually, that isn't very champion-like behavior, now that I think about it. Not entering doesn't mean they're automatically as good as me, does it? I'm not being very fair to myself if I'm saying they're champions without even giving myself a chance to compete against them. So, getting back to my point . . . I am the one and only champion for the most part.

How does it feel to watch me beat these other fisher-men? [Cheering]

Feels pretty good, right? If it feels pretty good, let me hear you say "Yeah."

[Tell crowd you can't hear them, even though they say "yeah" pretty loud.]

I can't hear you! Let me hear you say "Yeah!"

[Let them say it again. Raise up your arms and then put one arm down, leaving one up to wave to the crowd as you walk offstage.]

After registration, we jockeyed for a good starting posi-tion among all of the boats and then blasted off into the sunset to spend the night catching largemouth bass. I kept thinking of nine A.M. the next morning, when we would put our boat in line with all of the other boats, and weigh our ten-fish limit; there would be the presenting of the jumbo-sized check, an acceptance speech, and then my new life would begin. The only thing to think about now was the "catching fish" part of the dream.

After blasting into the sunset and never looking back, we found ourselves far from anyone at all, and at our first spot, I caught a bass that was probably a hefty four pounds. Perfect. An incredible start. Nine more like this and our two-man team would win, and I would be a star. I put the fish into a well in the bottom of the boat, as pro tournament regulations mandated that you keep fish alive so they can be released later. I made another cast. Thirteen hours till the weigh-in. Something to note here: Delirium becomes a factor when floating on water in complete darkness except for ultraviolet lights. So, at some point in the middle of the night, it felt like we were drifting alone in the dark and hearing dead men singing disco songs under our boat. We explored the most remote reaches of the lake, far from anyone or anything, looking for more fish that would bite. Trees in isolated coves that would be photographed for calendars or postcards on any given sunny spring day became the psychotic wooded habitat of devils slaughtering goats while naked women sat idly by and ate cake in overstuffed chairs next to dead cats in the soft glow of our ultraviolet lanterns. The lanterns that were officially guaranteed not to scare fish were officially scaring the hell out of me. Occasionally we would open a couple more Cokes and drink them with a fistful of M&Ms or Skittles to help us stay awake, and we would make some small talk to pass the time.

"Dan, would you hand me my sweatshirt from the back of the boat?"

"It's not a goat. That devil thing made it out of rugs and dirt clods, I think. Trying to fool us."

Hour number nine of our little night fishing tournament was as close as I will ever come to being in a swamp in Vietnam on acid dreaming of my bed back home and worrying about hiding the whites of my eyes. I had just further thinned my blood with Coke and candy when I looked up and saw something that had made its way off the shore and was somehow sort of levitating a few feet above the water about ten yards away.

"You see that?"

"Yep. Good sign," said Bill.

Wait. Think. Bill is one of them somehow. He is a visitor. Oh, is he ever. He is V. He has been waiting to meet them here on earth, and he talked me into being here fishing with him because they need a human to test or to tame or to take away. I wasn't going to crack.

"Go to hell, Bill. I'm not the one, man."

"Relax. If he's fishing here, it means there's fish."

Ah, right. Yes. Of course. I would not be taken aboard after all. It is only a boat, but not just any boat. It's the boat of a favorite pro of both of ours. The Joe DiMaggio of bass fishing, this guy. A bass-fishing tournament god. And how strange to meet out here at this hour after everything I've seen tonight in the black lights. I'm not even sure I'm in the mood for small talk.

"How you guys doin' tonight?" God asked.

"Not too great. We caught one way back around sunset, but that's it so far."

"Well, we'll find 'em biting before the sun comes up if we keep lookin'."

Those words may be the most sage advice I've gotten to this day. They come to mind in the toughest times of my life when I can't seem to find what I need. Whether it's money or relationship problems or any of life's little tests that we all endure, when the answer seems to be further away than ever, with no chance of showing up, in life's darkest moments, I think of those words. *We will find them biting somewhere before the sun comes up if we keep looking.* It should be noted, however, that we didn't find them biting anywhere before sunrise, so I also think of that.

We only weighed in that one fish. And it had died, so it was worth even less because they dock you for that. And we sort of had to endure the shameful stares of a bunch of pro bass fishermen who endorsed catch-and-release conservation at almost any cost, and who failed to see the humor in my trying to make the fish appear to be still living, by means of acting like I couldn't hold on to him because of his vigorous efforts to flip about.

I walked with my one lone dead fish from the boat to the scale while every pro on the West Coast watched and our parents waited patiently in the crowd of onlookers. Of course, the pros all had a good number of fish to weigh. And of course their fish were alive and didn't have to be animated via spastic hand movements and faked slippery struggles. They all had been doing this awhile, and one of them here today would appear on the cover of a magazine with a larger-than-life check for catching fish. And the only check waiting for me would come next week, regular size, in a business-size envelope, for counting and packaging the lures that they used to catch it. Turns out you start off as an amateur and spend years working your way up to pro. I just stood there sleep deprived, giving up on trying to make my fish appear to be still alive, and thinking to myself, One of these days I'm gonna find something that doesn't take years.

A VERY GOOD FRIDAY

On a bag of plastic worms, there is something called a header card. It's the cardboard with a hole in it that allows the bag to be hung on a retail display rack. Inside there's just blank white space where it's been folded over at the factory. One day, I wrote and signed Ricky's name on the inside of a few before folding the card over, stapling it, and sending it on its way to retail. If you were a bass fisherman buying plastic worms in the mid-eighties, you may have found one of these gems:

"I celebrate sexual diversity!"
—**Ricky Pelson**

"Negroes are also God's children!"
—**Ricky Pelson**

"I am a pretty doll created by our Lord."
—**Ricky Pelson**

"When the world gets too crazy, I like to curl up with a good book and some soothing tea!"
—**Ricky Pelson**

(I stole the last one from a box of herbal tea.)

FANTASY INTERVIEW WITH MY HIGH-SCHOOL GUIDANCE COUNSELOR

HIM: So these are just some basic questions that will give administration an idea of how we're doing in the department. How are you, by the way? It's really good to see you today.

ME: [A little stunned by how nice counselor is suddenly being to me] I'm . . . uh . . . fine.

HIM: Okay, let's see . . . [Reading from a card he held in front of him] Do you feel you were given adequate advice on career direction during your visits?

ME: Well, you know . . . I basically was told I should man a fire lookout or be a ranger for the National Parks Service.

HIM: Good . . . and let's see . . . Do you plan on pursuing these plans and/or this direction of study after graduation?

ME: I told you I wasn't so interested in that. I'm not much of an outdoor type.

HIM: Uh-huh, so then . . . Do you feel that your test profile led you to a viable career option?

ME: I told you then that the test seemed a bit broad and general. I prefer to work alone; I have weak grades in math and science, good grades in photography and drama. I'm not sure how the test arrives at fire lookout personnel or park ranger based on that profile.

HIM: Right, but then we discussed having to sometimes photograph the fires. And having to employ acting skills in order to remain calm in dangerous situations both as a fire lookout and a ranger. Do you remember that?

ME:

HIM: Remember?

ME:

HIM: Can I assume you're agreeing that we arrived at a viable option for you in the testing?

ME: I'm afraid I can't let you fill that one in as a "yes" on your little card there.

HIM: But you said yourself that you—

ME: How have you been doing in your exit reviews with other students?

HIM: Very well. Pretty well. I mean . . .

ME: Do you think that maybe you're better suited for something else?

HIM: It's important that we stick to the review form here.

ME: Because you're much more the outdoor type than me.

HIM: Me?

ME: Absolutely. The weekend camping. The scanner in your office to listen in on late-spring forest fire developments and search-and-rescue dispatches.

HIM: Yeah . . . well . . . it's a little late for me
    to be thinking about a career change.

ME: Absolutely not.

HIM:

ME: Think about it . . . a park ranger. Maybe
    even the fire lookout thing, who knows?

PARADISE HIGH BOBCATS DAILY
BULLETIN REVISED

- Thought of the Day: Bobcat Image is what *other
  people* think we are. Bobcat Integrity is what *we*
  think we are. The Bobcat Clawing Feeling in
  your stomach is the truth . . . and the truth is
  killing you.

- Tonight is the Yearbook Dance. The dance is
  from 8–11 P.M. Tickets will be sold at the door
  only. They will be $3 with ASB, $5 without. If
  you're thinking lots of Jack Daniel's and Pepsi,
  then trying to consummate unrequited crush on
  usual cheerleading suspect who is well out of your
  league, we suggest budgeting somewhere in the
  twenty-five-dollar range. Your twenty-two-year-
  old loser friend in the trailer will buy you the
  ten-dollar booze, taking five for himself to buy
  second-rate porno and off-brand smokes. You'll
  need one ticket at the five-dollar "lost my ID"
  price, and you'll be worked for five bucks' worth
  of "gas money" by whoever gives your sorry,
  unpopular ass a ride home to pass out alone. The

Pepsi you will have brought from home, since for some reason your parents are still kind enough to always make sure there's plenty in the fridge.

- Attention, athletes: All spring sport pictures are in the Student Store now. Please pick them up before we box them up. There are no pictures of loners, only athletes, so freshman and sophomore misfit types can continue hanging out on the stairs and thinking about esoteric things like professional bass fishing and nurturing the denial that is keeping you alive. Don't fight instinct when it attempts to preserve you.

- Yearbooks are on sale in the Student Store at lunch—$55 with ASB, $65 without. Take the yearbook around to classmates so that they can write things in it like "If I see you at the lake I will kill your lame ass." Sharon Wilson has written this in your yearbooks every year since the eighth grade.

- Calling all Drama Club and Thespian Society members: Our final meeting of the year will be held Friday, June 1, at lunch in the Drama Room. Snacks will be provided, so come eat, drink, and stand around lying about how talented you think each other are. Be sure to keep in touch so that in fifteen years, after you're tired and broken in ways I can't describe in this daily bulletin—mostly from sleeping around with forty-something-year-old so-called producers of always-rejected television pilots—you can all become rehab buddies for those six to eight court-mandated weeks in Phoenix, Arizona.

- Seniors: Remember to return all books to the library. You must return books, pay fines, and clear your record with us before you can graduate. By now you've all heard the story of the freelance writer living in New York who can't even look an editor in the eye and say he has a high-school diploma . . . all because Mr. Smart-Ass refused to square up with us.

3

University

I didn't really have the grades to get in.

PICKING A SCHOOL REGARDLESS

First choices

Yale (Lit or Drama)

Harvard (Business)

Backup

Butte Community College, Oroville,
California (1.5 semesters of general education
requirements. Pay with money order unless
they take Discover Card.)

4

Ending the
Ten-Year Hiatus

and Starting That Career
in Rock and Roll

Look at the green podium with the goldish-yellow bobcat on it. It's that kind of yellow that's trying hard to be gold and falling short; I believe its called goldenrod. Hear what they are saying about this evening and the future. This is the first day of the rest of your lives, they say. The big bright futures are starting right now. Ah, finally, you think to yourself in your neat little green gown, even though the evil valedictorian inside of you is saying something different. He is giving a speech of another sort, one in which he tells you to look into the audience of siblings and parents, and to pick out people who you know graduated from this high school four or five or however many years ago, then ask yourself if anything bright happened to them on the first day of the rest of their lives way back then. "Hey, look!" the evil valedictorian says in your head. "It's the guy who used to make varsity every year and now makes bathtub crank in a single-wide mobile home just outside the county line. He pushes the stuff to washed-up bikers at the Tic Tock Lounge so he can make a little dough on the side. And wasn't that guy next to him arrested sitting in a car he had broken into in the church parking lot last year? Yeah, something about indecent exposure. Might have been a suicide thing, because there was something about him trying to asphyxiate himself, too." But you don't let this speech inside your head get you down. Instead you tell that little voice in your head to shut up. Everything is fine. When you tell the evil valedictorian in your head to shut up, this is a big gesture . . . because part of you believes him. Part of you even kind of likes him, and that part would maybe rather be hanging out under the bleachers and looking for the warm six-pack that either one of you might have ditched there before students and families and faculty arrived to start talking about how bright the future is and how your life is going to change after this. The very first incredible thing about the immediate future that happens to you is finding out that the little scroll/cardboard tube that the principal is handing to all graduates is empty. You seem to be mildly confused about this being intended in any way whatsoever as a gesture meant to mark the beginning of a full life and future after high school. Empty + first day of rest of your life = bad hunch about future. And when I look down at the vacant scroll/tube thing in his hand in mild disbelief, it feels like everyone in the bleachers is suddenly clapping *at* me, not *with* me . . . sort of like drunk patrons at the local steakhouse who get a kick out of a tray of glassware dropping. And I know I am screwed. But I like listening to the faculty and valedictorians speaking. Because, as suddenly as June, they are mentioning us in the same breath as advances in medicine, the first men to embark on space travel, the forefathers of our country, and the boy from one town over who has a lazy eye and nerve damage to his left arm from a motocross bicycle racing accident but whose spirit remains unbroken and who was still able to secure a football scholarship to a nearby state college. It's too good to be true. Only months ago these same members of the faculty scowled at me anytime something went wrong and said something like, "You think this is hard? Wait until you get to college," implying that I had *nothing* in common with astronauts and presidents and the motocross bike racer/state college football player. But not tonight. Tonight is the end of those days, and tomorrow is the very first day of being brighter and more incredible.

The next day when I wake up, everything feels pretty much the same. I'm lying in bed feeling like blind optimism's regrettable one-night stand. Like the future woke up hung over next to the likes of me, rolled over, and kind of thought, Okay, think. What's this guy's name, again? Oh, God. What was I saying about him last night? Something about being just like a president or astronaut? Man, last night . . . that was crazy talk.

As days go by, incredible things are not happening.

Not in the good sense, anyway. I mean, I do think it is kind of incredible that everybody I know is leaving this town. My friends are leaving to go to college. My parents are moving to another small town about an hour and a half down the road because my dad has taken a job with a newspaper there. My sister is already off to college. I am the only one with nothing going on, and so I just kind of figure I'll move with my parents out of default. Maybe they won't notice that I don't have much else going on.

"So, have you given any thought to what you're doing?" This from my dad.

"Yep. Some, uh, pretty big things."

"You have a lot of opportunities that I didn't have when I was your age, you know."

"Yeah . . . it's all, you know, pretty great." Pause. "Hey, do you think it would be okay if we sold my bed at the garage sale so I could have a futon in my room at the new house?"

Long pause.

"Give your mom a hand bringing the groceries in."

When we get to the new house, I set up my room exactly the same as it has been since the eighth grade, to lessen the anxiety of being disoriented by change. I wake up in the morning, and my dad is already off to his new job at the newspaper. I roll over half awake, drop my arm down, pull on one of the nautical little handles to open a drawer on the bottom of my captain's bed, and reach into where my underwear and socks have been stored since the eighth grade. The captain is now eighteen years of age. I grab a pair of each and head off to the shower, trying not to think about the way my new life is unfolding, and that outside of this house is a new town bordered by miles of flat tomato fields punctuated with county roads and grain towers and by the northbound side of the interstate, which leads right back to the day I graduated. Trying not to think about the fact that the only person to hang out with today, once again, for the second week, will be my mom, and that I will once again end up helping her with decorating and making household craft items designed to quaintly disguise the more unspeakable household sundries like tissues and toilet paper. I think about how some people simply don't hit their stride until a little later in this life, and so, maybe I just need something to kill the pain of today while I wait, and wait, and wait, and wait. Maybe today when I'm busy helping her make kitchen plaques by affixing faux-antique canned fruit labels to small squares of stained wood, I can distract her long enough to sneak a burning and bittersweet, long, thick gulp of the semi-toxic clear varnish used to give the plaques their very authentic-looking finish. Maybe the varnish is my painkiller.

No. This is stopping. Or changing. It has to. Today I will make something happen. At least I will find a job in this town. I know there has to be a video store. And this afternoon I will drive until I find it. And I do. There, by the 7-Eleven store, near the railroad tracks, is the video store. And the parking lot is full of drunk workers from the tomato fields who duck into the 7-Eleven for large cans of beer one or two at a time, and then before leaving the parking lot after their postwork party, head into the video store and rent something. And let's face it, if you don't speak the language, and you're working in a field filled with round red tomatoes from about six A.M. till three, and you've had a few beers in the hot, sunny 7-Eleven parking lot by, say, three-thirty in the afternoon, and your wife is far away back in the old country . . . that rental tape will be porno. Plus, the other clue is that when they come out of the store, they always hold up a bag with a tape or two in it and wave to their buddies who are still finishing beers and say some kind of words, and while I don't actually speak any Spanish, the words sound sort of sexual to me, and their buddies all start laughing and cheering. One of them catches my eye while I'm sitting in my truck in front of the store watching all of this, and I kind of give him a little wave and halfheartedly return his cheer. He jumps up and down on the bumper of my small truck a few times and they all start laughing and whistling. Oh, man, maybe they think I'm some kind of parking-lot boy-hooker thing. . . . Was that supposed to be like he was humping my Toyota truck? Okay, so now I kind of have two options for work. Now I'm actually a little overwhelmed by the fact that only this morning I felt like I had nothing, and now at three-thirty, I feel like I can either be a hooker or a video store clerk, so I start the engine and drive around aimlessly weighing possible schedules and hours in my head. I just keep driving, not really caring where I'm going, just thinking and trying to stay out of the new bedroom, and avoid another day of craft-making and lying on a captain's bed staring at the ceiling. The hot valley sun, and the smells of hot vinyl upholstery and fields of fertilizer close in around me as I drive. Wait. Look at this place. A long string of ware-

houses. Is this what the future feels like? When the valedictorian said "wide open," he may have meant these
wide-open parking lots for warehouse employees. When he
said "bright," he might have been talking about the mid-
day sun shining down on the bright white concrete of the
outdoor employee smoking areas with one to three gangly
aluminum picnic tables sitting in the center of them like
some kind of huge, shiny metal grasshopper that landed
there when he jumped out of the grayish-green exhaust-
stained bushes that tried to grow between the parking lot
and Interstate 5. The metal grasshoppers stayed there
frozen as if they couldn't believe their good luck for having landed right on the fifteen-by-fifteen concrete square
next to two five-gallon buckets of sand, cigarette butts,
and gum. I decide to check the warehouses out, since now
I have my video store/parking-lot boy-hooker work options
and can check out other opportunities without feeling like
I'm under pressure. I survey the newfound land, driving
slowly along the endless line of warehouses, craning to see
what is behind each warehouse door.

- **Behind Warehouse Door #1:** Buckets of something
  that might be car wax or some kind of fuel
  additive, judging by the race-car/checkered-flag
  logo on the loading bay door.
- **Door #2:** The sides of motor homes. No middles,
  backs, or fronts, as far as I can see.
- **Door #3:** Hair-care products, and the employees
  are making a game of slam-dunking leaky and
  damaged bottles of various products into a large

box marked *Rejects*. For a second I think this is a sign and that this is the place. And then I drive past and peer into the next warehouse.

- **Door #4:** Music.

I see the Warner Brothers logo on the end of a long aisle of storage shelves, the same logo I have seen spinning on turntables since I was old enough to listen to records. Holy God, this is a sign from above; I have hit the sweet, sweet paydirt. I drive a little closer to the loading bay door. There are more records and tapes than you can imagine. Suddenly everything seems clear to me. The ten-year hiatus is over, it's time to return to music, and I have hit the mother lode. I can work here for the money to get the Les Paul guitar. The break is over. I'll make enough dough here to even buy recording equipment to make a demo, and someday my own record will be on these shelves. This, I think, is as close to a religious experience as I am ever going to have. I stand staring at the large blank outside wall of the warehouse, knowing that inside there must be endless aisles of maybe every record ever made. Through the loading bay door, and way back into the cool and deep warehouse, I can barely see the shadows and silhouettes of a wonderland of people pushing little carts that they are putting the records into like Oompah Loompahs working in Willy Wonka's record factory. I get out of the small mottled truck—whose paint, since we moved here, has been for some reason peeling off in sheets about the size of a newspaper folded in half—and I stand staring. Valley heat and the faraway smells of something rotting to make tomatoes grow bigger mix with Interstate 5 exhaust, and I am feeling like I have bought the Willy Wonka bar with the golden ticket. I'm ready to step inside and take my free tour of the factory that will change my life forever. But first I need to muster the confidence to walk in and ask for a job application. It won't be easy just walking in and letting them know I am supposed to be here and that something bigger than me has brought me here—it will take courage—but that's what dreams take. Right? (Answer is yes.) I will do this. I walk west past the loading bay door, following the large, cool, blank concrete wall of the warehouse until I see a small glass door. I push the glass door. I push it again. No luck. The receptionist in there is signaling somebody, waving frantically to somebody I can't see. Wait. Me? I push once more and at almost the same time kind of jar it twice back and forth really quickly to try to open it, shoving and even pounding the edge with the palm of my hand to . . .

Oh.

Okay, never mind.

Pull, is what she's saying.

I pull the door to my dreams and it opens with ease. I step inside and let the air-conditioning wash over me as I take a minute to catch my breath from trying to open the door.

"Sorry about that. I couldn't tell what you were saying to do."

She doesn't hear me, even though she's looking right at me? Deaf/hearing-impaired person? Ah, headset. I start to work up the nerve to ask for an application, but before I can, she motions toward a stack of applications and pens on the desk in front of her. I make a mistake on my first application, so I get a new one without asking, since there are around fifty or so in the stack. No big deal. She calls a guy in to interview me and the interview goes well.

"Yes . . . yes, I am able to lift up to fifty pounds. Also, um, more than fifty on occasion if need be."

He hears this and checks a box on my application and then continues with his questions. He starts talking again, something about needing to repeat something, but I really don't catch it. . . . I'm busy thinking about how much I can really lift. When I snap back to the interview, he's saying numbers. Maybe somebody's phone number or something? I really can't tell.

"Eight, three, oh . . . two, six, four."

"I'm . . . not sure I . . ."

"Just repeat the numbers to me."

"Okay . . . well, you said two . . . there was a two in there. Also, you said fifty when we were talking about lifting things. I offered to lift more, and I was thinking of the number seventy-five, but I don't believe I said the number seventy-five out loud."

"One more time. Listen closely. Eight, three, oh . . . two, six, four."

Pause.

(Going through my head: This is somehow a trick, or a problem or an equation. Think. What is he trying to tell you? Do something with this number that will impress him. Divide it or something. Show him that you're thinking. You can do this. No, you can't. You never listened or learned in math class. You only barely remember when they said something about how you would use long division in your day-to-day adult life and you were a smart-ass and you laughed inside and now here you are. Now you're not laughing, just like the teachers said you wouldn't be laughing one day. Okay, calm; just repeat the numbers before you forget what they are. That might be your only chance. Hurry. Now. Fast.)

"Eight, three, one, two, six, four!"

"Great. Just not so fast."

"Oh. Right."

"Remember to build that little pause in there. The person pulling the records from the shelf has to hear you clearly. So it's eight, three, oh . . . two, six, four."

"Ayyyyt . . . threeee . . . ohhhhh . . ."

"Well, not *too* slow. We have a lot of big orders to pull on most days."

"Okay."

Turns out, I aced it. I start tomorrow at nine in the morning. As I'm walking out, I can't help but wonder if the tests for college may not have been so hard, after all. Okay, forget about that now . . . I have finally landed exactly where I'm supposed to be, and it won't be long now.

It's my first morning at my record industry (warehouse) job, and the magic still hasn't worn off. Everybody seems happy here. Well, everyone except this one guy. This guy is the only guy in the whole place who doesn't seem to have the magic happening. He asks me if I want to buy some weed, and he asks me if I want to get in on a situation where cases of product are left at the back loading door and replaced with an envelope of cash by some guy driving a Datsun hatchback. He tells me his name is Hank. I politely let Hank know I'm fine on both accounts, and he seems to understand and decides to take a minute to let me know which of the women in the company he would make love to, given the choice between all of them. This is interesting to me, because this guy is not exactly residing in the traditionally handsome file. He is, really, even disqualified from the more forgiving untraditionally handsome file, mainly due to lack of personal hygiene and, as I'll discover, a taste for T-shirts that are decorated with cartoons of men getting drunk and saying funny things like "I don't have a drinking problem! I drink, get drunk, and fall down! No problem!" or the equally popular "One tequila, two tequila, three tequila, floor." When he looks down at his chest and reads this one aloud, his index finger follows along, and he always replaces the "Three tequila, floor" part with "*Weed*, tequila, floor," and makes a mimed gesture of smoking marijuana when he gets to that revision. This one cracks him up. And these sayings on the T-shirts are the sayings he weaves into his everyday conversation, and that's kind of his whole schtick. He's popular with two or three loading bay guys, and a little bit popular with me since he talks to me and I'm still new . . . and because I am somehow impressed with the self-confidence required for Hank to assume there may be a point in time, no matter how hypothetical, when every female working here might simply decide in unison to make themselves naked and available to him in hopes of being chosen for sex.

The way things worked in the warehouse was that you paired up with another employee and one of you was the person who pushed the small cart thing, and the other person walked ahead, pulling down the records and tapes corresponding with the numbers that the cart driver called out from a computer printout order. And this was how my favorite records became a series of bar codes and numbers dictating the title, format, and quantity of each. I was mostly getting stuck pulling orders with Hank, so, socially, things were only going to get better for me if I could somehow get away from him and make friends with the others and make it clear that I wasn't friends with this guy. It felt like a small betrayal. But I had to muster the confidence to distance myself from him if I was going to get ahead and make more money in the business, so I could get the equipment I needed to get back to making my music dreams come true. And so my days were spent trying to figure out who to talk to about not working with this guy and making my way through the maze with him time after time and day after day. And then I met the manager of the order department.

I was trying to remember where she placed on the "Guess who I would make sweet love to" list. Pretty high up, if I recalled correctly. She was pretty and had gorgeous blond hair and was maybe six or so years older than me. She had good taste in music. One afternoon, I saw her taking a break near the vending machines, eating a small foil packet of Lorna Doone cookies and drinking a Pepsi. She was the only one near the vending machines, as most of the other people were taking their break outside by the interstate on the concrete smoking square. I didn't smoke, so I made my way over to the break-room, where the vending machines were, to "coincidentally" enjoy a snack item with her, even though I didn't have any change since I hadn't gotten my first paycheck yet, and was more broke than when I was nine. I stood in front of the machine with my back to her, acting like I couldn't make up my mind which snack I would buy with the money that I didn't actually have. I shifted my weight back and forth and tilted my head at a few different angles, all of which was intended to convey indecision over vending machine snacks, and after an agonizing six minutes, I was wondering if this was working when suddenly . . .

"Do you want one of these cookies? I can't finish them."

"Oh. Hi. I didn't see you there. Yeah . . . sure . . . I was going to get some of those, but I was looking to see if there was maybe a smaller pack. I work out, so . . . you know . . . I try to only have a certain amount of . . . food."

"What do you do?"

"I work here."

"No, I mean what kind of workout stuff?"

"Oh. You know . . . different . . . machine type of . . . free-lifting Nautilus things, basically."

She just kind of smiled for no apparent reason as I ate my cookie, looked around the room, and generally kind of relaxed on my break. She even talked again.

"Do you like R.E.M.?"

"Great band."

"Because the label gave me tickets to see them tonight after a listening party for their new record, and I can't find anybody who wants to go to the city. Do you feel—"

"Oh."

"—like going?"

"Okay."

After work we were to drive about an hour and a half to San Francisco. I explained to my parents that I would be home late because I had a "work thing to go to." Listening parties were when a record company would rent out a big hotel room, decorate it with posters of a new record, stock it with various (free) drinks and trays filled with small food (also free), and then play over and over again the record that was displayed on the posters around the room. And during these parties, sometimes the pop star or group who made the album that was on the posters and playing over and over again on the portable stereo would also be in the room having drinks and small food right along with you.

We stood in the room and listened and ate and drank over and over again. We went to a concert and listened some more and watched. I even had a chance (somewhere around free drink number four back at listening party) to hint that I wasn't hitting it off with the guy Hank I was getting paired up with. My manager/date said it would be taken care of. And we went home. And these nights in San Francisco hotel rooms with posters and small food and records and then concerts happened again and again and again . . . and then . . . my manager was my girlfriend. And I was teamed with new people in the warehouse, and at night and on the weekends, our little group of friends would make it to these parties or to the beaches in towns like Petaluma or to concerts or almost anywhere in the world as long as we could drive there within about an hour from the small and flat tomato farming/industrial manufacturing town that we were all living in. And in my new world everything was free. Free pizza when we worked late in the warehouse, free drinks and food at the parties, free posters, records, and tapes, and once CDs came out . . . free CDs. No rent at my parents' house. I was rich. I went around the maze of records and tapes in the warehouse with the cart maybe fifteen times on the average day, five days a week, so around seventy-five times a week, three hundred times a month. For the first thirty-six hundred times around the maze, life seemed good to me. It seemed like things were maybe changing, and I was finally getting close to music. Sure, between working in the warehouse and going to parties in hotel rooms, all of my time was spent, but at least I was buying some of the musical equipment I would need to make a demo tape and live my dreams. But then somewhere around the six thousandth time around the maze of aisles of records and tapes and orders and numbers, life started seeming like some kind of rut or routine, as if I was going around and around in some kind of maze or something. Music became numbers, the aisles became days, the weeks and months became warehouses that held days, and I was getting tired of going in circles and always winding up back at the same place. Everything inside of me was saying it was time to quit, even though I was still falling short of having rekindled my music-making dream. And then something happened.

I saw a job posting.

They needed somebody to write and lay out the weekly advertising mailer that was sent out from the company to all of the music retailers around the country. And the newspaper where my dad was working was throwing away all of their advertising clip art and getting computers, so I drove the peeling truck over to their offices and threw as many of the ad slicks and clip art files as I could grab into the back, then drove home and stayed up all night faking a portfolio full of corporate mailers that I could bring into work to make it seem like I'd been doing that type of thing all along. I did a fake corporate newsletter for a popular tire manufacturer, because I found tons of clip art of truck tires. I did some made-up company fliers for parties, because I had a whole folder of glossy black-and-white mugs of beer. I went in the next morning in one of those button-up shirts from a department store—the ones that have some kind of name different from the actual department store's name (Weekendz by JCPenney? Cosmopolitan by Mervyn's?)—which I always think will change things somehow, with my portfolio, looking like I had stayed up all night drinking my parents' Taster's Choice freeze-dried instant coffee. I reported to the office of the woman who was hiring for this new position. She was the creative director.

"Hi, Don. How are you?"

"Dan, actually."

"Right. Are you on your break?"

"Yeah, but I'm actually bringing in my portfolio for the job producing the weekly mailer."

"Oh, I didn't realize . . ."

"That's okay. Not a lot of people realize that I write and design corporate mailers, brochures, newsletters, and announcements."

During the interview there were no numbers to

memorize. She asked me questions about what I want to do, asked me "what my passion was." I kind of kept the music thing under my hat, because I was afraid it might undermine my new passion for designing mailers and newsletters.

"I'm one of those kind of people that only does what he is passionate about. See, so it's kind of weird, you asking me that, because I just showed you my passion for designing and writing the graphic design pieces."

I got the job and even had my own little office. Gone were my days of laboring. Now I was creating, and laying out, and lettering and bordering and shading. I was even hiding little subliminal messages to my ex-manager but still current girlfriend in the mailer advertisements, a tiny word or phrase about where she and I might have gone over the weekend, or what I thought of the album, or maybe a secret nickname that only she knew and only she would find hidden in busy photographs of stoic pop stars on album covers. And there were more tickets and backstage passes, mainly as a result of making friends with the representatives from record labels who would come into my little office to drop off marketing materials and ad slicks, gay men in their late thirties and early forties who I flirted with (doesn't mean I'm gay) for concert tickets. I mainly told them that they had really nice eyes or that I liked what they had done with their hairstyle. And only when nobody was within earshot. It means I would do anything for rock and roll, is what it means. I'm sure. You think it means I'm gay? Oh, man. Wait. I bet there is a kind of gay where you have sex with women, and you don't have sexual feelings about guys, but technically you are still gay. Oh, there is that kind of gay, I bet. So what. Whatever. I didn't say the thing about the eyes and hair to just anybody. Bill from Warner Music, yes. But have you seen Bill from Warner Music's eyes? They're blue enough to comment on, you know, without sounding like you're hitting on him. Look, I don't have to explain this to you. Quit looking at me with that closed-minded look on your face. One year later, Bill and I were married in a very spiritual, but not legally binding, ceremony in Marin County with close friends and family looking on just one month before the U2 *Joshua Tree* concert tickets went on sale. I will never be able to thank my working-class father for his understanding. I will never be able to thank my rather startled girlfriend for her understanding and support. I'm lying. My point is that I wasn't just whoring it up with anybody who walked through the door, I was only, you know, committed to building something with a very select group of middle-aged male sales reps. There was Steve from Polygram, for instance. I never led Steve on. I had no desire to see any of the bands on his label.

"Hi, Steve."

"Wow, looks like I have to start dropping by the ad department more often if they're gonna start hiring hip young guys to design our ads."

"Yeah, my girlfriend and I went away for the weekend and we were lying in bed and she was telling me that there was a job in this department. So I went for it. She's great. A guy like me would be lost without a girlfriend, Steve. Ah, the beautiful, sweet women that I love, Steve. I love them and . . . I . . . um . . . make sweet . . . beautiful . . . um, love . . . to them.

Looking back, I realize Steve was probably a little creeped out by the guy who designed his ads and managed to turn every casual greeting into a mention of having sex with his girlfriend over the weekend.

As the year went by, there were more listening parties than ever. And it was at these times that I felt so close to my recording career finally having arrived. There I was with the posters and the beer and the small food items and the hotel and the girl. . . . The only thing I really had left to do was continue buying recording equipment and instruments with the money I was making, learn how to operate the equipment, learn to write some songs, record those songs, get those songs to a record company, and then have the record company like the songs. So, you know, except for that stuff, I was pretty much there. I was finally close to my pop-star fantasy lifestyle of hit-single success: I had some money in my pocket, and I was dating the twenty-seven-year-old manager of the shipping department. I was spending most of my time at her apartment, but also a couple of nights a week in the replica of my eighth-through-twelfth-grade bedroom, which was slowly becoming filled with drum machines, amplifiers, and other things I figured I needed but didn't really understand yet; the best of both worlds, really. Sort of like Keith or Mick splitting time between an apartment in the city and a house in the country, except instead of London, both the apartment and the house were in a very small and flat tomato farming/industrial manufacturing town on the outskirts of Sacramento, California. But something stopped working, or more accurately never really started working. I was never getting around to writing and recording songs, even though I figured I must've had all of the equipment I needed (?).

I had stacks and stacks of manuals that had all of the operating instructions for the equipment I had been buying, but I never had the time to read them. I was only nineteen and going to an office twelve hours a day every day. The few times that I did fire up the drum machine and run it through some of the speakers stacked up in my room, and then figured out how to plug one of the guitars into the mixing board and run it through another ampli-fier, then tried to program the synthesizer's electronic horn section and orchestra to play the same notes I was playing on my guitar while I figured out how to get the drum machine to play right . . . my parents made me unplug it all because of the noise.

And the months ticked by, and it was always some-body else's record I was advertising, and it was always someone else's listening party we were attending, and no matter how much closer to the stage than the rest of the audience we were at a concert, I was never going to be stepping out there. Okay, no problem. I'd make a few adjustments and get on with it. I broke up with my ex-manager girlfriend very suddenly in the parking lot of a lunch spot, in an attempt to finally focus on making my recording career happen. I spent all of my free time in the evening after work reading instruction manuals and still failing to learn how to work the drum machine and fake computerized orchestra strings. No matter how much I read, nothing seemed to work. The computerized drum-mer was a spastic and violent quitter prone to just stop-ping in the middle of a song, and the fake and lazy orchestra always came in late and tired or drunk and somehow out of tune. And now, as if advertising, celebrating, and selling everybody else's record at work all day wasn't bad enough, I had to watch my ex-girlfriend/ ex-manager and her new boyfriend from the warehouse hang around being happy for eight hours a day, and even leaving for parties and concerts and weekends at the beach together while I was headed home to try to read instruction manuals written by Japanese people. And I realized at age nineteen that no matter how close I found myself standing to what I really wanted to do, after faking my way halfway there with a bunch of shortcuts, I was still a million miles away from actually doing it.

So I made another move. I moved out of my parents' house. I got my own apartment and dedicated myself to my music. But I was caught in a quandary because work was still getting in the way all day.

No problem.

I quit my job. I would get by somehow. This is how dreams happen. People ask you how you plan to get by without a job and you look out to the horizon and kind of get serious and a little bit cocky and you say something like, "I really don't know. But I'm gonna make it happen, man." But soon I was caught in another fix. Rent and bills were coming due all at once and I had kissed my job good-bye and had not become a pop star yet. No problem, I would sell whatever I had to stay afloat. But the, uh, only stuff I had that was really worth anything was . . . my . . . music equipment. No problem. I would sell my music equipment to pay my rent and bills while I worked solely on my music. I was focusing on music all day, but each month I had a little less equipment to work with until finally I had nothing left. Whatever. I still had learned at least one valuable thing. If I can pass it on to one person out there, then my failure was worth it in the long run. It's this:

SOMETIMES IN YOUR LIFE, YOU HAVE TO FIND A LONG, PAINFUL ROAD.

Wait.

EVERY TIME YOU NEED PAIN, YOU HAVE TO FIND A LONG ROAD AND WALK . . . AROUND, AND THEN HAVE SOME DREAMS. OR SOMETHING.

I can't remember the one valuable thing that I want to pass on to one person right now. It was something I had read in my horoscope the day I sold my last piece of equipment and headed back north on the interstate to where I started from. God, I hate that. What the hell was it? Whatever. I'll remember. It'll come to me.

LOOKING BACK:
WHAT I WOULD'VE SAID IF I COULD'VE BEEN VALEDICTORIAN AT MY HIGH-SCHOOL GRADUATION CEREMONY

Okay . . . hello.

[Adjust microphone]

Well, Paradise High School Bobcats, you've done it. You've taken the first step into the future with your big bobcat . . . claw . . . or hoof or whatever bobcats have. Foot? Yeah, maybe just *foot*. I think that's what bobcats have. If we were the Shasta High School Eagles, we would have talons. Keep your eye on those guys, they're going to have maybe even brighter futures than us. Think about it: They can fly, they have really good eyes that can see miles away, and they have razor-sharp talons. I've never really thought about it until just now, but the Shasta Eagles might be a little better off.

Okay. What was I saying?

Oh. Right. Some of us will step out there with our bobcat foot and become bobcat doctors who help others and make advances in medicine. Some of us will go out there and become bobcat lawyers, defending the rights of others and the Constitution of this country. Some of us will even become bobcat parents and have little bobcat . . . calves . . . or bobkittens or whatever those would be called. I don't really know that much about wildlife, but what I'm saying is that some of us will have children. Still others of us will be some other kind of bobcat, one that doesn't really fit in with the other types of bobcats I've mentioned here this evening. Maybe a "sleeping in and eating a little too much bobcat" or maybe a "staying in my parents' house until they ask me to leave and hopefully by then I've figured something out bobcat." A lot of us are already planning on going away to college. Others are finding a place in their family business. Still others of us are thinking about maybe moving along with our parents to a small agricultural town near Interstate 5 on the outskirts of Sacramento and maybe trying to record some music with electronic equipment, or just working at some kind of part-time job. Good. Very good. It's important that we know that those are *all* good plans.

[Get a feel for crowd and cover at least half of the following.]

The Future
- Actually special or just as good as present?
- They said that by 1984 everything would be all really sci fi/futuristic. Obviously did not happen.

Tonight
- Safety stuff about drinking and driving.
- Who is *not* going away to college? (Ask for show of hands.) Let's talk after ceremony and exchange phone numbers.

Inspirational Message/End
- Famous authors who did not publish until late in life/didn't "plan" to do anything.
- Sports analogy: "Not over till it's over," "You can't spell TEAM with ME" or however that one goes.

FAULTY LIFE PLANS DEVISED AT ROCK CONCERTS IN THE LATE EIGHTIES

At an Oingo Boingo Concert in Davis, California

Danny Elfman has not worried about anything and somehow everything has worked out fine for him. This man I am watching onstage is the man I should be more like. He has not gone to a university to study music, yet because of an intense passion for his work and the ability to put himself out there without regard for what critics or peers might think or say, he is here playing songs, and there are even motion picture scores and soundtracks for him these days. He is successful on what appears to be his own terms. Therefore, starting tonight, I will never go to a university to learn how to compose music for motion pictures.

At a Replacements Concert in Santa Rosa, California

Do you think Paul Westerberg or Tommy Stinson ever worried much about the fact that they were just a couple of kids from the middle of nowhere? No, they didn't. They never gave it enough of a second thought to keep them from winding up here tonight playing these songs. They drank and played and wrote songs in the middle of nowhere and have wound up very far from where they started out. Tonight they will get on a luxury tour bus and continue touring and enjoying their work and the rewards of it. Okay, then: As of tomorrow I am going to drink in the middle of nowhere.

At an R.E.M. Concert in Sacramento, California

Man, these guys are good examples. Just be who you are. Just be yourself. I seriously doubt it was ever a "cool" thing to be singing about "spiriting a rattlesnake" and some old man named Wendell G or "perfect circles of acquaintances and friends." But look at these guys, up there onstage tonight with all of these people here to see them. And they have just been themselves and never tried to be anything else. That kind of humble confidence with just being who you are will always lead you to success, no matter what your pursuit. I need to start being more about rattlesnakes and, like, spiriting them or whatever he says in that song. I should get myself an old-man friend with a cool name like their guy named Wendell G that they're singing about.

5

Medium Suicide

Every now and then in our lives, something works out. Maybe it's right in the middle of a long line of years' worth of things that don't really work out so well. And maybe it's not the thing you're planning on or looking for, or even the thing you're going to stick with for the long run . . . maybe its only purpose is to make you realize that not everything you do is bound to fail. And maybe you find it accidentally, without even looking, while working at a health club on the outskirts of town across the highway from the volume-driven, membership-based discount grocery warehouses. And at first it seems like something that you could never even do. Maybe it's fighting forest fires when you're twenty-three years old on the Mendocino OC 27 type II hand crew.

"But how would that ever come to be?" you ask.

Well, maybe you're living in a small town not far from where you went to high school, and maybe you've somehow managed to get a job at that local health club that has weights and a swimming pool and racquetball courts. You know . . . it's the old thing where you take the job because after quitting your job in a warehouse filled with records and tapes and then selling all of your music equipment to pay your rent but then winding up broke and right back where you started, you could use the money. Maybe the job is the type of thing where you're washing the towels, folding the towels, answering the phones, filling the Powerade machines, and greeting the guests at the front desk when you take their membership card and give the requested number of towels. Don't worry or feel awkward about any of this. Believe me when I tell you that it's totally normal. I should know; I went through the very same thing myself. I know what you're thinking. You're thinking, Why would I have a job opening this health club at five-thirty in the morning when I'm just this really skinny, unfit, smoking, drinking, confused person who doesn't even work out, stays up late, has a problem getting up before ten in the morning, and eats mostly prepackaged snack foods served in a tavern that smells like urinal cakes and has only a toaster oven for a kitchen? Well, the answer to your question is this: Because sometimes you have to do exactly the opposite of what your instinct tells you to do if your aim is to change your

life and reinvent yourself. And also, because your physically fit sister is a friend of the owner and has convinced
them to give you a job. And also, because the staff is
mostly college students who cannot work the 5:30 A.M. to
9:30 A.M. shift five days a week, which kind of shows you
how sometimes college can just get in the way (Bill Gates
dropped out) of good opportunities, right? Is your little
job at the health club the thing that I'm talking about
when I say that every now and then in our lives, something works out? Is it the thing that shows you how not
everything you do is bound to fail? Probably not, judging
by some of the first things that happen while you're working there. For example, there's the incident of you waking
up an hour and a half late, jumping out of bed, not having
the time to shower or comb your hair, pulling on your uniform of white shorts and a green short-sleeve knit sport
shirt that has the Kangaroo Kourts logo on the right
breast pocket and your name written on the left breast in
iron-on letters . . . the kind from those little shops in the
mall where you can make a shirt say something like
"Happy Birthday, [NAME]!" or "My child is a student at
[NAME OF SCHOOL] and is an often tardy, poor speller
who is marginally driven by the frustration of mild
dyslexia and who thinks it's cool and funny to live like a
goddamn teenage drifter on a steady diet of bargain-
brand beer, and gas station minimart hot dogs, and cigarettes bummed from so-called friends even though he has
a family who loves him." Anyway, that was not such a
good morning, and it occurred a little too early on in your
tenure at the club to not be duly noted by the manage-
ment. But they are kind and forgiving to you, as so many

people have been. And even though the healthy, early-
rising, ambitious, and successful clientele who pay their
steep monthly dues on time had formed a small angry
mob at the front doors by 5:45 A.M., tempers had cooled
down by the time you rode up on your secondhand motorcycle in your little white-and-teal uniform looking like a
B-list, hungover daredevil who lost or pawned his helmet
and cape. It was at about 7:08 in the morning when you
rode up on your little Honda 250, which couldn't go fast
enough to win in a race against panic and guilt. The
organic rice and instant grains mogul from the next town
over who swam in lane four every morning at 5:30 A.M.
sharp let you slide. This meant a lot to you, as you kind of
looked up to the organic rice mogul and his brothers.
They seemed to have it all figured out, these rice men
from generations of rice men. The extremely perky aerobics girl who seemed trapped behind a smile that barely
concealed her contempt and turned her violent currents of
obsessive perfectionism, day-old half-price hate, and flow-
ering disdain, which was planted maybe decades ago at a
lonely prom, into manic cheer and a bubbly disposition
also let you slide on this early misstep. And the guilty and
shamed muscle man with the porn-star mustache who
was always smelling of the cigarettes he sneaked in the
club's parking lot between sit-ups and weight lifting knew
enough about mistakes to just smile and calmly wait as
you parked your motorcycle by the door, panicked for a
sleepy second when you almost knocked it off the kick-
stand by getting your shorts caught on the stupid back
fender when you tried to get off the damn thing, and then
backed away from it slowly with your hands and arms

extended in front of you making that "Staaaay" gesture. You used your employee key to open the doors, followed by your special Allan wrench type of key to secure the doors into the open position. And so now, with your biggest mistake out of the way, you were free to hold the job for your standard stint of six to nine months.

You must be a very proud young man.

Yes, this is your time.

You have arrived (late).

My drill was pretty much the same each morning when I opened the club. I would get in at around 5:15, open the doors, and then let them lock behind me, in case any of the extra-eager early-bird let-me-show-you-how-happy-and-successful-and-driven-I-am-by-getting-here-at-five-twenty-in-the-morning-to-start-my-five-thirty-workout-and-not-only-am-I-here-earlier-than-the-early-opening-time-but-I-am-happy-and-you-can-see-that-by-the-great-big-smile-I-put-on-my-face-and-you-can-tell-by-the-things-I-say-like-"Good morning, I feel great today, don't you?"-and-when-I-say-these-things-I-am-reminding-you-that-I-will-succeed-because-I-am-willing-to-do-things-like-this-and-you-clearly-are-not-and-that-is-okay-as-a-matter-of-fact-it's-more-than-okay-I-actually-feel-kind-of-sorry-for-less-driven-people-because-they-will-never-know-the-success-that-I-am-clearly-heading-straight-for-like-a-human-arrow-headed-straight-at-a-great-big-imaginary-bull's-eye-on-the-horizon-that-I-am-kicking-in-my-six-A.M.-step-aerobics-class-and-that-is-one-bull's-eye-that-you-cannot-kick-my-friend-because-you-are-not-me-and-when-I-look-out-of-the-big-glass-windows-of-my-step-aerobics-class-you-are-leaning-on-the-counter-like-a-tired-

bartender-and-you-can-barely-hand-people-their-towels-
let-alone-kick-the-imaginary-bull's-eye-of-success type of
people should try to sneak in before the club was officially
open. Then I would turn on the lights, using the switches in
the breaker box, and it was so early and so quiet that you
could hear the usually pleasant and unobtrusive suburban
fluorescent lights buzzing like mad. Maybe even buzzing as
if they thought this was a stupid time to be awake as well.
I don't even think wildlife is awake at this time in forests or
desserts or whatever. Coal miners and army men probably
sleep later than this, even. Then I would walk through the
men's locker room and make sure that the soap and hair gel
dispensers were full and there were no old towels left lying
around from the closing shift people. Take the footstools
down off the lockers. Then go into the ladies' locker room,
where the naked ghosts of the female club members whom
I had secret crushes on would dance around in midair like
an R-rated version of the haunted house at Disneyland,
and they would float by having naked-girl towel fights and
giggling. And I saw all of this in my mind on sort of bad
eighties video footage with way too many hot spots in the
lighting, and the naked-girl ghosts cast shadows where
there shouldn't be shadows, and occasionally a green, blue,
and purple wavy line obscured my seeing the more revealing and explicit moments that the naked ghosts indulged
in, just like on the unscrambled Playboy Channel. It was
the same drill in the women's locker room to make sure it
was ready for business—dispensers full, footstools down—
and then out to the pool area to reel back the big blue cover
that lay on the water overnight, revealing the light blue
swim lane waters lit from underneath. Then I would kind

of stand there looking down at the water and up at the early-morning dark purple sky with stars still there for light above this suburban-sprawl dead-end abyss, watching the reflections of the water on everything stucco on the very outskirts of this town. Over the fence, a gas station. Across the highway, a strip mall next to that larger-than-life super-discount grocery warehouse. Looking at the water and feeling for a split second like maybe I should jump in and swim to the bottom and look for a secret way out of this place forever, like in those movies where somebody is trapped in a seaside cave's air pocket because the tide has come up when they weren't paying attention at the beach and now the only way to escape is to dive deeper in to somehow find a way out. You're dozing off! Wake up! Okay, time to straighten my uniform, put a little of the complimentary hair gel from the locker room in my hair, and get my ass back up to the front counter to mix up a big bucket of lemon-lime or orange Powerade for the drink machine. Oh, and get some clean folded towels up on the counter and unlock the doors. Take the membership card, give the member a towel, answer the phone. Say hello, thank you, and good-bye.

Repeat.

After my shift was over at 9:30 A.M., I would go home and sleep until I went out that night to drink pitchers of cheap beer with fast and equally cheap friends. Play improvised drinking games in small bars where we would never pay to hear the local punk band playing in the next room. Maybe steal a case of bagels from the bakery out by the train tracks or blow up large milk shakes with firecrackers in the Jack in the Box parking lot, or just break into a downtown beauty supply shop and steal two wigs to wear while we drink whatever we still have left. Maybe mix it with something like orange Tang shoplifted from the 7-Eleven. And every day was going that way. And eventually the people through the big glass windows of the step aerobics class were starting to get to me. They were doing something with their lives. The more I watched them, the more I realized I was clearly *not* kicking the big imaginary bull's-eye on the horizon. I was *not* marching in place to the beat of the MC Hammer song. I was *not* stepping up to the plate, much less stepping up, spinning around, clapping once, stepping back down, and getting ready to really feel it in my thighs and buttocks. I decided to try a medium lemon-lime Powerade for free (allowed to). I was kind of thirsty and hungover from staying out the night before and the night before that and the last fifty or so nights before that night. "Shiny Happy People" by R.E.M. came on the radio. Michael Stipe sang the line "Meet me in the crowd," and it felt like one of the signs he'd been singing to me ever since that second R.E.M. record, which had the song "Radio Free Europe" on it where he said to me, "The Sunday shelf hip radio's got a steak(?)."

Okay, I'm not sure what he says or if any lyrics on that record were a sign to me, but this new song of theirs seemed to be speaking to me. And it felt good just leaning up against the counter, listening to the song, drinking my powerade, and watching the shiny aerobics people and the happy weight-lifting people. Then I had another medium lemon-lime Powerade, a large orange, two more medium lemon-limes, something called a health nut muffin with

PROtein, and one small lemon-lime for the road since my shift was almost over. I was feeling good. I was feeling unstoppable, but I needed something to push me over the edge of feeling and right into actually doing. I mixed lemon lime and orange together in a cup the way I used to order cherry-and-Coke-mixed Slurpees at the 7-Eleven when I was younger. It's called a Suicide when you mix them. So I peaked with a medium Suicide, and I was feeling every part of the muffin. *I will not sleep. I am not about sleeping. I'm not even sure I feel like going home.* Everywhere I looked I saw the imaginary bull's-eye on the horizon. I was feeling very "on." Pumped up, I think they call it. Yeah, pumped. I wanted something to happen, man. I don't know if it showed on the outside, because most of the stuff I feel or think never really shows up on the outside. I think all it looked like on the outside was a tired, hungover skinny guy leaning up against the counter staring at the aerobics class, drinking something out of a wax paper cup with various athletic equipment company logos on it, and waiting for the last ten minutes of his shift to pass. A customer came in and gave his membership card. It might have looked like business as usual, but the fact is, I was pumped and psyched. He put in his towel order.

"Can I get two sweat towels?"

"Let's do up it."

"What?"

"Never mind."

I don't care if he heard me or not. He heard me. If I said that, he heard me say it. There. I just thought that about what I said, which is completely different from saying that about what I thought. Man, I can think clearly on this stuff. I thought that . . . just now. I didn't say that. I know. I know. I know. I know. I know. Sounds weird if you say it long enough. Has anybody ever thought that? Is somebody thinking that right now? How many other towels are being touched right now in the whole world? Okay, how many *yellow* towels? Riiiiiigggght . . . now. Sort thoughts. Last thought not important. Prior thought not important. First and sixth thoughts only important thoughts in sequence.

Clean up unnecessary thoughts and fragments?
Yes.

```
ARCHIVE ITEMS NOW.
DON'T PROMPT ME ABOUT THIS
AGAIN.
>
>
>
C:\ POWERADE
C:\ START
```

This stuff was clearly bringing out the best in me, and this girl named Kalie, who's a trainer on staff, came in around 9:25, just like she did every day. She would hang out at the counter with me and we would talk while I waited for the nine-thirty to one-thirty counter person to come in. She was really hot and I have no idea why she always hung out and talked to me for the last ten or so minutes of my shift as opposed to just heading into the weight room or the office that the trainers would use to get ready for meeting their clients. She usually talked to me about problems she was having with her boyfriend. I was that guy, apparently cast as some genderless and asexual slacker/eunuch whom she could talk to about her relationship problems without the worry of driving her personal stock down within her circle of girlfriends, and without wrecking the chance of a potential score by talking about relationships to a guy, since I clearly wasn't the potential-score guy. Mouth opens. She talked and I drank the 'ade. Total time spent talking: three minutes, ten seconds. List information conveyed below, sorted by relevance. Insert bullet-point format.

- Hi.
- Can't believe ten o'clock appointment canceled, now has to stand around re-alphabetizing stupid client workout cards and clean the Nautilus machines.
- Her and Mark having problems again.
- Going to break up for good this time.
- Fire season is starting and (she) is still training to be a smoke jumper.
- Third summer she's been on a crew and they don't see each other for the whole three months.
- She is proud that she is strong enough to be on a crew.
- (He) kept mentioning that he had lunch plans on Saturday.
- Lunch is with ex-girlfriend.
- Ex is a hooker.

- Okay, stripper.
- Kalie believes that in God's eyes hookers and strippers are same thing.

She finished her talking, and I had managed one more Powerade while extrapolating and sorting the pertinent information from what she was saying. I finished thinking, sorting, and drinking. Why would God be thinking about hookers and strippers? I think he just sees us as people. It would be kind of creepy if God was sizing women up and setting aside strippers and hookers into some kind of categories like, "Yeah, I think she's a stripper. I mean, at least she could definitely be a stripper if she wanted to be, if you know what I mean. She's almost too pretty to be a hooker." I threw the wax paper cup away after I crushed it with one hand, and in my head I heard James Garner deliver the *Rockford Files* line about how they stopped making tin cans years ago in favor of aluminum and now everybody can be a tough guy. I love that line because my sister loves that line, and I file that line in its appropriate area in my brain and am ready to reply to Kalie.

"How do I get signed up for that? I wanna do that."

"It's gross for guys. Trust me. Women do not like a guy who strips for a living."

"Forest fighting or whatever. Fires. Forest-fire fighting."

"You should start training here! Start lifting and running and then take the fire science courses. I could totally get you all the information. This is my third season."

After my shift, Kalie started a client card for me with all of the suggested sets and weights and reps and speeds and stretches and times that would transform me. For the first few times, I would get done with my shift and take my card from the file and follow my routine to the mark, crossing off sets of tens with lines in two groups of four and then the final slanted fifth line that made it five. At the end of my workout, I would file my card back in the stack, hit the shower, change, and then head across the highway to the super-sized discount grocery warehouse and buy some name-brand high-protein egg substitute, fresh fruit, and juice. I would go home and make a big protein breakfast. It didn't last long, this newfound system and order. My attitude had started to change as my body started getting a little bit bigger, and by week three, I realized I didn't need the little blue client card and the egg substitutes as much as I just needed to be lifting as much of the weights as I could during my shift and then washing down protein muffins with the antifreeze-colored Ade of Power. My system was simple: Eat and drink behind the counter, where it was free, and then anytime I walked by some weights in the club, heave and pull and yank and lift on them. Whether it was on my way to answer the club guest courtesy phone, or to replace a burned-out lightbulb, or to take a bathroom break . . . whatever barbell or machine I walked by, I would just get my body under it and shove it into the air or set it on the heaviest setting I thought I could budge and yank on its ropes and handles or levers a few times on my way past it. An important part of the system was staying jacked up on the sugary sports drink. I was mixing batches of it twice and three times in a four-hour shift. I was like a speed freak cooking batches of small-town-biker amphetamine, albeit a speed freak in a neat little white-and-green sporty uniform that had my name on the breast. So, maybe not as badass, but still. I started getting paranoid. Goddamn manager. Asking too many questions.

"Wow, really selling a lot of Powerade, huh?"

"Oh yeah. Yeah,yeah,alotofit,man. Andprotein-muffins,man. That'scool,though." (Fast, nervous laughter until I realize manager is not joining in.)

"Are you ringing food and drink on key five maybe by accident? Because your snack sales are still the same."

"Keyfive,keyfour,keythree,keyseven. Whateverkey, man. Whatkey? Whichkey? Whoknowskey, man."

And if the manager kept pressing for details, I would ask to take my five-minute bathroom break, then take a fast walk through the club, lifting and yanking and lurching and heaving almost anything I walked by that looked like it was heavy. And the physical part of this was working. There were lumps and lines and shapes on me where there had been nothing but a skinny, quiet geek before. One promise was finally coming true for every sea monkey that never grew. For every pair of glasses that never let me see through a girl's clothes or even through my skin and to the bones of my own hand, I was finally starting to see something happen. Oh, the bittersweet citrusy taste of growing from boy to man, which I will never forget. And in what felt like a huge mix-up in the administrative offices upstairs, I was selected as employee of the month. Portrait hung up in the lobby, my own parking space for my little motorcycle, a little write-up in the newsletter.

There was, however, another component to all of this that had nothing to do with the suburban health club that now had a stiff and awkward portrait on the wall of me in a mild state of disbelief. There was the fire science reading and testing and qualifying. And the freeway was the only thing that stood between me and the small and barely funded community college where one obtained his wildland fire suppression certification.

I had to get out past where the suburban sprawl ended or at least took pause, out to the open fields under the huge buzzing power lines, and there I could read and listen and test. I was smart enough to know that at seven in the morning, getting the little Honda 250 up to freeway speed would mean it would be cold even though it was already early April. So instead of shorts and a T-shirt, I put on a sweater and a pair of cords, figuring that this was the appropriate cold-weather gear for something like this. I filled my leather portfolio/binder left over from my days of producing the weekly record company mailer with some notebook paper, bungee-corded it to the back fender, and was ready to go. I snaked through the usual little surface streets that led past the health club and out toward the freeway. And then, as if my little motorcycle were a horse reluctantly learning a new turn in the path, I turned it toward the freeway on ramp that it usually rode right past, getting the bike up to speeds it had never really felt before. Second gear done, third gear done, fourth gear . . . Holy God, it felt like we were going maybe 104 miles per hour. Water was streaming out of my eyes as I strained to look down at the speedometer. I saw the red needle and I couldn't believe the number it was pointing to. Forty.

What?! I'm only up to forty? Oh my God. Holy Christ, I need about twenty-five more miles an hour to even fit in at the end of the on ramp. I twisted the hand-grip throttle thing as far down as my frozen and shaking arm could twist it. More water was coming out of my eyes, and now also very thin snot from my nose. Oh my God, I was barely inching toward fifty miles per hour when the snot started. What was going to happen if I got her up to sixty or seventy? All I wanted to do was be able to look like I was casually flowing into traffic by the time I reached the end of the ramp. You've seen cars and motorcycles do this before on freeways every day. At fifty miles per hour, I realized something was making the bike sway and jerk hard to the left. It was my right knee. I was slamming it involuntarily over and over again into the side of the motorcycle. Why was I doing this? Oh, I must be really cold. Jesus, that explains not being able to make a tight enough fist on the handle grip thing to twist it harder. It felt like right when you wake up and you can't make a fist to open a jar of instant coffee. Here comes the end of the ramp. I looked in my mirror. Apparently there had been a small car, a Chevette or Pinto, behind me all along, and the driver, a sixteen-year-old girl, was flipping me off for not going fast enough. Not going fast enough? Jesus, that's easy to think when you're in your Chevette or Pinto car behind all of your luxurious glass and steel. Fifty is hauling ass when you're out here in it, sister. Trust me.

After a long ride along the freeway's emergency lane, I was at the exit for the community college. Oh, sweet . . . I could slow down now. Slowing down was not a problem and all of the motorists would see this. At the end of the ramp I made a left and started riding the cycle up the long, winding two-lane road that led across the community college campus. Okay, now comes the redemption: easily maintaining a speed five miles an hour *faster* than the posted twenty miles per hour campus speed limit. Doing twenty-five in a twenty, buzzing right past the small parked cars that seemed like big predators swooping down on me only moments ago out there on the freeway. Casually nodding hello to the community college students who were smoking cigarettes next to their tired and wilted early-eighties economy cars.

I parked my motorcycle and grabbed my handsome leather executive binder from the back fender, and I made my way across campus. What? I can barely walk. Oh, man . . . It was like my legs had fallen asleep. Come to think of it, the last thing I even recall my right leg doing was slamming into the side of the cycle repeatedly and involuntarily about ten minutes after starting the early-morning cold commute. I guess it took a while to get this contorted, and now the thawing would take a while as well. I walked with a limp and drag that looked not so much like a cool sports injury, but rather like some kind of mild degenerative bone condition or muscle atrophy. It must've looked like God was making a little miracle happen right there at Butte Community College as the twenty-two-year-old, apparently bedridden, mildly disabled boy hunched and scraped along, dragging his leg right along with him and making his way toward the running track and football field. Yes he can. Go get 'em, tiger. We're going to have a very special little forest firefighter with us today.

When I got inside, I was surprised by the size of the turnout. After checking in, we were taken to a larger, more permanent structure and seated in this lecture-style classroom. There was a man telling us what forms to get off the desk, how to fill them out, and what we'd be doing today. I dragged my leg to the front desk and forced my hands into about thirty-five percent of a closed grip when grabbing the forms and a tiny number-two pencil. There were some tears left on my face, maybe. Most of the snot had been wiped onto my sweater and, I hoped, was drying clear. In some kind of "coincidence," the man at the table with the forms and tiny pencils made an announcement about physical limitations just as I was making my way back to a seat about halfway up the stadium type of seating arrangement, clutching my forms and papers to my chest with my right forearm. As I scraped along up the stairs to find a seat, trying to look casual and not stressed about whether or not anyone could see the snot on my sleeves, he said loudly from behind and now below me, "If you have any physical limitations or disabilities, you should not be applying for ground-crew work at this time. Please see me and we will get you forms for dispatch or other positions open in your district." I tried to have a look on my face that said I was thinking about other things as I hunched and pushed my way up the stairs and to a seat. I sat down, and there in the seat in front of me, facing away from me, was Kevin.

I was hoping I might skip the part of my life about Kevin. Kevin was a frustrated teen guitarist/shoplifter guy I ended up making friends with in the eleventh grade, after my professional bass-fishing goals fell by the wayside with the big defeat at the night tournament. He worked at the corner store near my parents' house and would set aside one large bottle of cheap champagne or two forty-ounce bottles of beer under the back steps of the store. After he closed the store, we would take the booze and we would walk around the tract-housing development that was brand new and still vacant, just walking and drinking in a pleasant ghost town of cul-de-sacs inhabited only by two minors not happy with the way things were shaping up so far and needing to have a drink and take a walk to size things up. The development was on its way to being a perfectly pleasant quasi-upscale suburban neighborhood for young professionals, but until the homes were sold, it was still a place where you could walk along the brand-new white sidewalks and little fitness park's exercise trails, taking slugs of discount champagne or malt liquor. After we were done, we would usually go back to Kevin's house. He would do some crank, explaining that he didn't have enough to share and that it was only so he could get eleven hours of guitar practice in before school the next day. I wasn't interested in trying crank, anyway. I figured I was already skittish enough, always laughing nervously at inappropriate times in social situations, so I could pass on it. But I felt good about being in the position of seeming hard core enough to be in the same room as the crank, without having to try it since there was only enough for Kevin to use as a study aid of sorts. I remember thinking that Kevin seemed like a doctor administering his own prescription, very sophisticated somehow and very gentlemanly. "Pardon me while I administer a few CCs of pharmaceutical cocaine hydrochloride . . . I have a lot of work to get done this evening." I would stick around sobering up enough to go home to my parents' house and, while I was there, listen to Kevin play the same scale or Iron Maiden riff over and over, sounding exactly the same each labored and stiff time but with more specific emotion on his face with each run-through. Kevin never really ended up doing much with his music. After a while he set it aside to live in L.A. without a car.

I sat down and spread my forms and papers out on the little desk attached to the side of my plastic chair in the permanent structure, happy to forget that other pursuits had not worked out for either of us. He let me get settled and then turned around.

"Rock star practice . . . fireman exams. What's next for us? Astronaut school?"

I started laughing so hard and trying to suppress it that I was kind of lurching, and my mouth was still sort of thawing, so I think there was some wincing and wiping with whatever clean space I could find on the sweater. This cued the man with the pencils and the forms to make his announcement again about people with "disabilities or limitations," and then we got down to business. The first thing we would be doing was watching a film about fighting forest fires. Excellent. I could use something to pump my confidence up after that freeway commute and then bumping into Kevin.

FILM'S TITLE:

Wildland Fire Suppression USFS Western Division 5

Film's Opening Montage

A young man about my age, bandaged up and sitting in a hospital bed, with most of his body burned, talking about how he's still going to fight forest fires, because it's in his blood.

(What?)

A forest fire races up the side of a canyon and burns over several abandoned fire trucks and an empty helicopter.

(Why are they ...)

A father is talking about having lost two sons to wildland fire fighting.

(I thought they would show us, like, the ...)

Aerial footage of huge burning trees falling and lines of ground crew racing out of the way of them.

(Why are they all, you know ...)

A whole crew hiding under foil blanket things while fire rages right over them, leaving them physically unscathed but understandably scattered and stammering.

(getting burned and . . .)

A man holding what appears to be one of the foil blankets all folded up in a square says, "Are you ready to risk everything?"

(What? No. Is this even the right movie, this movie they're showing?)

We sat through another fifteen minutes of wildland fire-fighting bloopers and then finally the movie started showing some stuff happening correctly. Oh my God. Finally. By the time we started seeing things go according to plan, I was wondering who the hell was running the show and why everybody was getting chased and burned. Oh my God. No wonder! All of the guys in the movie had the same seventy-two hours of community college training that I was going to receive. Okay, keep it together. Don't crack . . . that's what they're testing you on right now. Who's going to crack? Not me. I was kind of sitting there trying to put it all into perspective. I was telling myself that every summer job has its risks. I mean, just because I wasn't shown a movie about fifteen different health club employees dropping barbells on their necks, choking to death on protein muffins, or drowning in covered swimming pools at five in the morning with hangovers doesn't mean that my health club job was safe. When the film was over, the man at the front of the class turned on the lights, and Kevin was gone. There were other empty seats, too, and I was a little confused about the movie still but excited that I had stayed. The man used the same booming voice that he had used when he kept making the announcement about people with disabilities:

"How many people here are willing to be in any one of the situations you just witnessed?"

A trick question, right? Just say you're willing. Big deal, you're just saying it . . . you're not even signing anything. Obviously you're not willing to be set on fire for eighty-five dollars a day, but you want the job, so just act like being set on fire sometimes is fine. It's just one of those things you say in a job interview, basically. I wiped one last run of my nose onto my sweater sleeve and raised my hand. The man just looked at me and then kind of looked around the room, as if he was waiting for other people to raise their hands. Dammit. I'd raised my hand too fast. The man was looking confused as to what I was doing, like, maybe asking to go to the bathroom or something. So I clarified it by saying, "I will. I mean, do it, or whatever . . . risk it."

Turns out the question was rhetorical.

Whatever.

As days went by, I found rides to the community college instead of freezing and only going forty-five. I learned all about light flashy fuels, snags, old growth, lightning strikes, escape routes, box canyons, complexes, bad situations, air support, strike teams, good situations, tools, tool maintenance, hose packs, hardware, saws, radios, sawyers, line, cutting line, and drawing the line. I found out what it felt like to find myself passing one of the first written tests I had taken since that one I failed in my high-school guidance counselor's office about what I should do with the rest of my life. And then there was the matter of running a mile in time, and can you? Yes, it turns out. And then we'd go into the mountains for training and set fires and cut line, and can you do this? I thought, I can, yeah. And can you do this while these guys are screaming at you, telling you that you all look like girls? Screaming right into your face. Seriously? Like girls, you're thinking? Like that kind of intense thing going on behind everyday eyes no matter what pedestrian surroundings we find ourselves blending into? Like that thing where we're not only bubblegum "pop sexy" like Liz Phair or Nancy Sinatra, but serious and sort of "academic sexy" or "professional sexy" like the girl from *The Partridge Family* playing a lawyer on that TV show set in Los Angeles, all depending on the way we want to dress on any given day? Like that vibe of not only being able to live but to actually *make* life? To handle anything that comes up and almost never take a dent to the self-image? How is it that girls/we are able to be so humble and still so assured? Ah, that must be what the shouting men are getting at. We look like girls because we seem to be able to handle anything that comes our way in a humble and intelligent way and still be attractive . . . we're able to "put out fires" if you will? No, that's not what he's talking about, as it turns out. What the shouting man is now screaming is that "We cannot swing a tool without looking like somebody's mom." Ah, okay . . . not really *girls* at all. So, *women*, then. Then it *is* a confidence thing that he's getting at. He thinks we are a beautiful crew of self-assured trainees out here, is what he's saying. But quickly the line between his voice and every voice inside my head that screams at me about how things will never work in this life is thinning, stretching thinner still, and then, like a rubber band left for months on the dashboard of a car that your sister used to give you a ride in on your paper route, the breaking point comes when you thought it would stretch thinner still. The voices are outside and the voices are inside, at the same time. It's like the self-doubt has physically manifested itself out here in the mountains in the form of these screaming men in flame-retardant clothing.

- What the hell are you all looking up at the mountain for?
- You will never get up a mountain by looking up a mountain!
- Why the hell are you looking at me, you should be looking at what you're doing!
- You are going to kill the guy who's supposed to be covering your ass!
- If you guys can't handle it, then go back to the buses! Go home and cry!
- When the line says bump, you'd better move or you will be moved, if I have to move your ass myself!
- Let's go, man! Are you going to move this slow when the shit is going down?

The good part about being on the side of a mountain freezing your ass off and swinging some kind of ax thing called a Pulaski while guys scream the same things at you from the outside that you've been screaming at yourself from the inside your whole life is this: There is no

TV to watch, no bar to go to to ignore it, no three-to-nine-month girlfriend to tell you to just go to sleep, and no junk food or junk sex to lust and eat. And in a seamless, predictable, and wholly unbelievable edit in the mid-budget overproduced film of your life, the small training forest fire becomes a large real forest fire, and the same editor works his bad action-picture magic to make part of the group become your crew, and it's the middle of the night and you are somewhere in the middle of the Shasta Trinity National Forest and it's on fire and so hot you feel like you're melting in the scorching wind. This is the weather pattern they told you that the fire would create and that you would not see or feel until you were in the center of it. And out of the dark side of the forest, where there is no fire yet, there're helicopters appearing out of the black and dropping long strings of liquid fire from the sky to burn other patches of forest so that the fire in front of you doesn't move toward them and right over you, forcing you to deploy that silver fabric shelter hanging from your waist, making you feel like you're wrapping your own corpse and digging your own grave. This seems like a strange time to hear yourself thinking in a happy, suburban sort of voice not so unlike your mom's, "You know, every now and then something works out pretty well in this life." Then there's another moment altogether, on the last fire you go on for the season, in which very large flaming trees are falling on the mountain above you and racing down toward you like some kind of huge bottle rocket laid on the ground, aimed right at you, and then lit. Like God is somebody's big brother in the suburbs, bored and a little bit buzzed with a pack of bottle rockets, and he's laughing at almost nailing your ass and cracking up at the way you hop and scare to get out of the way. In that moment, I believe that if wildland fire fighting is in your blood, you are more alive and well than you have ever been, and even already looking forward to the next fire season. In my case, when that moment came, somewhere in the middle of Oregon at three or four in the morning after little or no sleep, after fighting the same fire for twelve long days, and at the end of the season maybe a day or two away from autumn rains that would take care of all of this, all I was thinking was, A hundred dollars a day *before* taxes? This is a rip-off. I should try something else. Maybe be a songwriter or something.

PITCHING THE SHOWERTEK™ FOGLESS
SHOWER SHAVING MIRROR

While I was working at the health club, fortune smiled on me, not because I'm some kind of good-looking guy America is used to seeing from the shoulders up on television, but because the local public-access cable shopping channel producer was a friend of the owner of the health club. And the owner said he and his crew could use the men's locker room shower as a location for free, and whatever employee was working when they showed up with their camera. They showed up to shoot it on a Tuesday morning around seven-thirty, so I headed to "the set."

TAKE ONE:
INT. HEALTH CLUB SHOWER—DAY
YOUNG MAN is in shower and fumbling with his
razor, trying to shave with a small fogged-up mirror
and acting out a painful sting as if he's cut himself
on the chin. Looks very frustrated. He will then be
shown discovering the PRODUCT.

YOUNG MAN

> There's got ... wait. Okay, turn off the
> camera. Hello? I can't see.
> You guys. Hello?

CUT!

They can't use that because I keep saying hello and
squinting and craning my head around trying to figure
out what I'm supposed to be doing. I'm told that I'm also
kind of whining, and that all I'm supposed to be doing is
simply looking frustrated.

TAKE EIGHT:
INT. HEALTH CLUB SHOWER—SAME DAY

YOUNG MAN

> There's *got* to be a better way to get a
> good, close shave.

Great. Cut. They can use this one. Now all that's left
for me to do is to be filmed (taped) using the product and
not saying anything. And so I move this along nicely,
because all it really involves is shaving my face for real, and

then all I have to do is get out of the shower, get out of these wet swimming trunks (Hollywood/Northern California production trick for shower scenes, it turns out), blow-dry my hair, and walk up to the camera, which is waiting outside of the locker room. Somebody will then say that I have a clean, close shave (a sexy female voice will be added in later, I'm told, but for now it will be the slightly overweight middle-aged man working the video camera saying this), and even though I don't care what he thinks of me, I can act pretty well . . . plus I think I'm actually pretty happy to hear that somebody likes my clean, close shave. So we get this one right off the bat. And then . . .

"Great. Let's do one more. And can you just chuck your chin when you look at the camera?"

"My chin? Act like I cut it again?"

"No, you're just kind of giving yourself a gentle punch on the chin."

"I don't really . . ."

"Just a soft, confident, like, gentle fist. Like, 'Hey, I'm a sexy guy.'"

"Like I'm thinking that you're a sexy guy?"

"What? Oh, no, no, no! Watch . . . like this . . ."

He steps toward me, still holding the big outdated video camera on one shoulder, and reaches toward my face with his free arm. I arch and bend back out of the way slowly, staying on my mark and avoiding his gentle, soft punch gesture.

He's frustrated that I outfoxed his move, I think.

"Fine, forget it. That's a wrap," he says.

USE MY MENTAL FOCUS TECHNIQUES TO
IMPROVE YOUR WORKOUT AT THE GYM

It should be noted that I am not a qualified personal physical trainer. However, I *did* work part time at a health club for a period in excess of four months and spoke with a certified personal trainer during that time. During that time I also made some mistakes that I don't want to see others concerned about physical fitness have to make. I will say this very clearly in case I did not make it clear to this point: YOU DO NOT NEED TO ABUSE LEMON-LIME AND ORANGE-FLAVORED SPORTS DRINKS TO AID YOUR WORKOUT. Trust me, there are plenty of natural ways to improve your workout performance. Maybe the best way is to use some of my Mental Focus Techniques™ listed below. Stay focused, say it out loud, and Get Pumped®.

Pec Machine
Overview of the situation: You're bringing these two padded sort of handle things together with your forearms from a seated position in order to lift some weights, and the weights don't really care if they get lifted up or not. Not very easy to get pumped up about this, is it? This is where your first mantra comes into play.

Say out loud: "Every time I pull these two pads together with my forearms, I am maybe smashing the head of someone I don't like so much between the two pads, and even though it is only two big, soft, fake leather pads that their head is being pressed in between, it is probably pretty clear to them that I do not like them and that I have some sort of grudge against them from the past and am using that to my advantage."

Bench Press

Overview of the situation: You're lying on your back on a so-called bench, and there's a bar above you containing some weights. You have to get excited about lifting it up and down, right? Right. About now you're staring up at the ceiling hoping for a miracle. Again, this is where my techniques come into play. If you can visualize a Real Good Strong Scenario® and say a mantra, chances are you're going to find yourself Naturally Excited™ about lifting this thing up and down. This one is a longer mantra and will require some practice.

Say out loud: "There is, say, one of my exes or even more, say, one or five of my exes sitting on the bar in between the plates of weight that are on either end. I can see that they are clearly glad to not be going out with me anymore by the way they are looking down at me and shaking their heads and rolling their eyes. They are telling me that they know there is no way I can ever lift this bar up and down ten or so times, and they are so certain I can't that they have promised to break up with whomever they are going out with now, even though that person(s) is supposedly stronger and more financially secure (and "ready to grow up," whatever that's supposed to imply) than me. All I have to do is lift this ten times today, and then do it several more days over the course of the next four months, and then we will get together and discuss how I am better than the other person and how we will go about letting that person know in a mature and adult fashion that it is over for him because she and I are getting back together."

Couch in Lobby

Overview of the situation: This is where you have ended up again, maybe after finishing working out, and maybe only after eating a few health nut muffins and barely even trying to work out.

Say out loud: "There are a million things I have to think about if I get up from here, so getting up may not be the best thing for me. As long as my mind can somehow sit here with me and not turn to bite like some kind of wired and scattered adopted pet with an undisclosed history, I will be fine. I can feel the fake leather holding me. It has come from some hot-metal warehouse in the central portion of just about any state in the country, where it made a lifetime of changing from one thing to the next. First, from a bucket of some kind of polyvinyl chloride–based goo into a huge piece of fabric, when it was spread onto some sort of cheesecloth type of backing. Next, from a huge flat piece of fabric into a long, thick roll of itself, being driven around by a forklift operator. And then finally stretched across a second-rate wood frame and stuffed to become this couch that is comforting me today. And the large-screen TV is showing a comedy that is set in and around a Boston pub, which was made in and around Burbank, California. And the actors bend off the edge of the large screen, as if no matter how hard they try to look and act like patrons and employees of a bar, they have wound up unbelievably stretched like this. But there's still something better about a screen this big, and the actors even seem more entertaining changed by the warp and bend. I don't know if there's really any reason to *try* to change or to *try* to work out. That's what the TV is telling me, basically. That's what this sweet, sweet, soft sun-warmed Naugahyde is teaching me. Why worry about weight lifting when the couch is teaching you that change happens quicker if you just stand or lie there? The bucket of polyvinyl chloride–based goo never *tried* to be anything, much less a sofa. And similarly, lying here with my reruns of *Cheers* and a four o'clock rusted California sun washing over part of my tired right arm and all of these "rent to own"–inspired surroundings and ambitions, I'm also not *trying* to be anything, and I'm excited about the change that this is sure to bring. And I'm happy to have the sofa and TV as proof that change occurs if you lie here and let it. Maybe TV and sofas are faith."

RE: FOREST FIRES IN NORTHERN CALIFORNIA

Willamette Forest, Oregon

You can hear the really deep groans and pops. And at night sometimes these deep wooden sounds of something two hundred years old and aching are accompanied by sparks when one of the popping sounds comes. The groans and pops are the sound of a really big tree burning from the inside out, usually after the fire outside of it has been put out. And on this night in the middle of somewhere in Oregon, where we are staged in the dark on the side of a mountain, you can hear the groaning and popping all over in the huge trees around and above us. When they come crashing down, it's weird, maybe one every few hours, because it's pitch black and you can't tell which huge tree is falling or where it's going to land. Sometimes they come out of the black above you, and after they hit the steep ground, they race down the mountain right past you. And when they do this, the oxygen gets inside the trunk of the tree and the fire starts raging away inside of it again and blasting out the back of it as it races by. They are almost always, somehow, by the grace of good luck and God, falling nowhere near our crew. And so tonight I'm almost lulled by the groaning and popping. And then suddenly one breaks just above us. I can feel the shake of it and hear it like hell, but I only barely see it coming, and it's hard to tell how far away it is in the dark. And then the oxygen gets inside and it's shooting a huge orange tail behind it and I can see that I should be jumping to the right. I do and it goes by. And now it's dusty and darker than it was before. I can't see an inch in front of my face. The crews spaced across this line are coughing and radios are crackling. We all get on our radios and say that everything is all right.

"Everybody all right?"

"Yep, all right."

What? Actually, if I can interject something here: Why are we doing this again? Does anything even live here? I mean, when it catches fire, all of the animals head out. I know this because we sometimes pass them running out on the roads leading in. So we aren't here to save them. And there's probably not any, like, super-smart miracle porpoise-like deer or bear that would come back into the fire and save any of us if we were pinned down and held smoldering here. Wait. Great, now there's a goddamn rattlesnake here. By me, dammit. This is what I'm talking about. It's, like, always going to be one thing or another as long as we're hanging around huge forests that are burning. It's like we're going out of our way to make our own problems if we keep doing this. Okay. It's okay, he's dead. I'm okay. The snake's dead. No problem. I'm good. This thing was cooked underground, I guess, and uprooted when the tree went. Well, actually that's kind of a plus. You can't really get bitten by a poisonous snake out here.

Mendocino National Forest, California

I love the crackers and jelly in our government-issue MREs (Meals Ready to Eat). I think my favorite entrée is the freeze-dried pork. And almost nobody seems to like the pork! I called Mark on the radio, and his guys are coming over to meet up with my guys on this side of the fire so we can all throw our MRE entrées in a pile and trade. Like a potluck kind of thing.

Shasta Trinity National Forest, California

Here's the thing: I know this is one of the best things I'll ever do or see or feel a part of in my life. And I'll wish I was back here, and I know right now that I never will be. Today we paired off in twos and headed down the side of a mountain along the edge of a canyon, setting it on fire like we were told to. These big flares that are in the side pouches of your packs. Fusees. You pull one out, strike the cap, and start pointing it at tree branches and the leaves and branches on the ground and anything else. And pretty soon everything you are leaving behind is roaring and it sounds like an endless rip of fifty thousand phone books being torn at once as you walk away. Jesus, finally a fitting metaphor for my twenties. Me and a guy I went to high school with who happened to wind up on my crew finally finding a way to be paid to wreck things. And later that night when I hiked up to the road to get hose hardware from an engine, I recognized the guy's voice in the dark and it was the drummer from my band in senior year of high school, well after the bass-fishing stuff didn't pan out. Weird how we've all wound up out here. Those helicopters came back dropping fiery strings of that napalmish stuff while Joe and I were burning that cut in the canyon with the fusees. Later on the Forest Service enlisted the help of local convicts when the fire started gaining ground. Common practice, we're told, when the fire is winning and resources are thinning or tiring. Me and Joe talked about what other community-based crews might show up. "Okay, we know all of you came to beauty school to get your cosmetology license and find yourself an open booth at the local Supercuts . . . but we need you. At ten-thirty tonight, you're all shipping out to a national forest that is on fire and is proving difficult to extinguish." We talk about starting a clown crew, contracting out as an additional personnel resource just like the convicts. We could just be independent contractors, and the Forest Service would never know we were clowns until we showed up at the fire in our secondhand ice cream truck painted with rainbows and clouds and things in really fun bright colors. We could hire small-town community college actors to be additional fire clowns with us. Cram maybe forty of us in the smoking, backfiring, dented-up ice cream truck. Everyone would hear us showing up at the fire with our loud carnival music playing through the ice cream truck's speakers. We would try to fight the fire with big seltzer bottles and always be tripping over one another in our huge floppy shoes. We could put smoke bombs in the back pockets of our baggy pants and get dizzy turning around in circles, scratching our heads trying to figure out where the fire was. And would any of these hand crew and convict crew guys really kick our ass? I mean, when it comes down to it . . . would anybody ever punch a clown? I bet not. We're just *talking* about doing it, and everyone on our crew is laughing already.

Lassen National Forest, California

When ten thousand acres of forest are burned through, the trees are gone and all that's left is white ash maybe a foot or two deep, as far as the eye can see. And then you send some guy like me walking across it with a walkie-talkie for a mile or two under a full moon, looking for what the more glamorous crew who was here when it was all going up in flames may have missed. I am walking in the middle of nothing. It feels like the moon. I am the janitor on the moon. Stuff hangs from my belt. I am equal parts Neil Armstrong and Mother Nature's cleaning man. The busboy. I am a mall security guard creature patrolling this strange lunar landscape. You cannot breathe in this atmosphere, but I can. And in the most beautiful gray and white full-moon stillness in the hush that comes when all that is left is miles and miles of canyon covered in two feet of ash, I am walking without making a sound except my breathing. My thighs and knees cut a silent wake through ash, feet and boots are out of my sight and somewhere deep down on the ground. Every now and then the other nature janitors call me on the radio and we all meet up to chop the hell out of a smoldering stump. This is not the exciting stuff they put in the training film. Everybody wants to fight fires, but nobody wants to be a caveman forest custodian cleaning up after it all.

6

Nice Shot, Tex

Just months before the alternative music scene exploded in Seattle, I cashed the last of my fire-fighting paychecks and used some of the money to buy an acoustic guitar. I also filled up the tank of my 1981 two-wheel-drive Toyota truck and drove. I drove for days—in the opposite direction of Seattle—all the way to Texas. Somebody had, uh, given me the tip that the alternative music scene was actually going to explode out of Austin, not Seattle. I should have doubted the validity of this tip, because as I made my way down the West Coast, staying with friends along the way, each friend I stayed with looked at me with this kind of blank, confused expression when I told them where I was going. Among the most popular responses from friends in L.A., San Francisco, and Tucson were:

"Why are you going to Texas?"
—Joe in San Francisco

"No, seriously."
—Brian in L.A.

"I didn't know you played that kind of music. I guess I didn't know you played music, period."
—Rob in Tucson

In retrospect, I can see that Rob had a point. The only bands I was in during my twenties never really got much accomplished. The reaction to my bands from audiences ranged from indifferent to violently opposed, as we could never play well enough to play any of their favorite songs. And any sincere attempt we made to do so was not well received—they usually thought we were making fun of their favorite songs. Basically, the only bands I was able to get by in were bands that when all of us played at once, with the volume high enough, you couldn't tell that I wasn't really much of a guitar player, and obviously didn't have much of an idea what to sing about. We once made the mistake of playing in a bowling alley bar filled with people who wanted to hear their favorite songs that the radio played. People who were "working for the weekend." Folks who couldn't "fight this feeling anymore," because at this point they had "forgotten what they started fighting for." We tried to fake our way through a few hit tunes, but clearly lacked the desire or know-how and pretty clearly (you suck) were not the favorite (can we turn the jukebox back on?) of the crowd. So, looking back, not being the best guitarist and singer to start with, I have to admit this decision to go solo and drive to Texas to make it may not have been the best decision.

After I got to Austin I found something out. I found out that with an acoustic guitar, and no wall of noise to hide behind, I couldn't really play any of the songs from the bands I used to be in. I also found out that I couldn't write a song. This was a problem, as I was lucky enough to have lined up a gig for the following night.

Okay, I thought. Don't panic. You came close when you were ten. Don't turn back again. Make this happen.

The first thing I needed to do was go buy a big amplifier for my Korean-made acoustic guitar to make it much louder. While at the pawnshop, I also bought a whole box full of cables and secondhand effect pedals to make the guitar "distort," "flange," "wah," "cry," and just about anything else I could make it do loudly. As for songs, I thought: Whatever. I can't worry about that right now. I'll make up the songs as I go along. That's how revolutions happen. You don't write and rehearse alternative music revolutions, you let them explode out of your angst-ridden, adolescent soul.

When I walk into the club in downtown Austin, the place is packed. I'm looking around, and everybody there is this awesome portrait of Southwestern music and song and life. I mean, these guys all look like country-folk legends. Their faces are etched in stone. They have long ponytails of gray hair. For the record, I am the *only* person in this place wearing cutoff army fatigue shorts and a flannel shirt with the sleeves cut off, and with very short hair that is not (yet) gray. Most of these people have their instruments next to them at the bar in black cases. Instruments. Not guitars, really, as much as smaller black cases containing the fiddle or mandolin that they will use to defy absolutely concrete laws of logic when they show you that you can be every bit as virtuoso as, say, Beethoven, and still drink and smoke and talk about the bass-fishing spot down the road. I mean, these men are playing songs that their dads and grandfathers played. Songs that have been alive for generations.

I make my way through this crowd in my second-hand army-man-goes-punk getup with about fifty pounds of secondhand electronic Japanese guitar accessories clanging around behind me. An amplifier in the case with the wheels on it. A couple of backpacks filled with cables and pedals that make the guitar able to do some things that I hope will impress the crowd. And of course a little journal that I've filled with notes on what I'm pissed off about, and/or what is going wrong with my life (girls and jobs) and/or the country (vague and confused corporation themes here) and the world (will try to leverage my limited understanding of foreign policy mostly). Those are the notes to try to work into the songs that I'm going to be making up on the spot.

And the best part is, I'm still not catching on to the fact that I'm in the wrong place at the wrong time. I mean, I've realized I'm very obviously the first one on the front lines of this revolution, but I still haven't started to kind of catch on that Texas is not the place where the revolution is happening. Meanwhile, unbeknownst to me, far away from Austin, way up in Seattle, bands are being formed, gigs are being played, people *aren't* being asked tons of questions by their friends about why the hell they're buying guitars.

And I have so much stuff to plug in and hook up that the sound guy tells me that in order for me to get my ten minutes to play, I have to start setting it all up behind the guys who are already playing. And I'm trying not to unplug the two guys onstage, who are busy reminding the audience that they are so adept on mandolin and fiddle that they can play flawless beautiful music and still not miss a beat or phrase when one of them leans down with an unlit cigarette in his mouth to get a light from a cute cowgirl in the front row. I think to myself about trying to pull that off, too, tonight. If not tonight, maybe remember to get some cigarettes for next time and give it a shot. They finish and everybody is clapping and it's my turn. I hit the stage and I turn on all of my stuff with that kind of casual urgency that rock stars take the stage with. I kind of act really casual about testing my equipment, using my feet to press the buttons on foot-operated effects like I've played a million gigs. It all starts to buzz and scream and howl through the club's speakers to let me know it's ready. I can't stop these things from shrieking, and I kind of act like I don't want to. I take a few seconds to act like I know how to tune my guitar, because I've seen enough concert videos to know this is something to do for the crowd. I act very, very particular about the tuning of the guitar and I suppose that looks very professional, but what I realize now is that what I was actually doing was delaying my inevitable failure. I can tune no longer because all of the effects that I've switched on are still making the screams and screeches and howling and buzzing sounds that seem to be getting louder the longer I take. I've apparently turned on way too much stuff, and even the sound guy can't seem to get all of it to stop from the back of the room.

I start trying to make up a song.

One . . . two . . .

These folks have no idea what to make of me. They aren't mean about it, but they are not exactly into it, either. I'm looking down at my little notebook and singing lines about the stuff that's been pissing me off lately while my electric sound storm is flailing around the room.

"You . . . uh . . . talk to your ex-boyfriend way too much on the telephone . . . yeah, I will wipe the slate clean . . . um, this revolution is here now . . . you'll just have to listen to me on the radio, won't you? Yeah, I will not . . . your capitalism is, um, FALLING DOOOWWWN!"

And I'm looking out into the audience to kind of see if any of this is hitting them. You know, see if the revolution is starting yet. These men are, like, looking at one another and trying not to laugh. As if I'm their little brother or their son and it's just kind of cute that I even got up there and tried. I try to play a couple more songs, and then wrap it up.

"Thanks for coming out tonight. I'm at the Cactus Café tomorrow night."

After the gig, on the way back to where I'm staying, I see a copy of *Spin* magazine on the newsstand. On the cover are the words "Seattle Scene Explodes." And here I am in Austin. I couldn't be farther away from where I needed to be, and I've spent all of my money getting here. So I get some odd jobs, make some money for gas and food, and make a plan to go to Seattle.

Nice.

NOTES ON DRIVING TO AUSTIN

#1

Late in the afternoon at the side of the road in New Mexico, I pull over to buy fireworks. They have everything here, and so I buy everything. I put bags of them in the truck. All of this only cost me thirty dollars! There are these really little things called jumping jacks that spin like hell when you light them. Twenty in a pack. They spin so fast that if they hit a pebble or something on the ground, they will take off flying through the air. There doesn't even have to be a pebble sometimes. Sometimes you'll have a few beers—say, maybe nine cans of it in a bar called the Cactus Café on the university campus in Austin. Then you'll be bored walking around campus that night, trying to figure out what to do with your life, and you'll decide to light four or five packages of them at once. And they will all seem to fly right into a wooden shed that holds stacks of newspapers waiting to be recycled. And no matter how far you reach your leg in through the hole where the people drop their papers in, and no matter how much you stomp your foot all around in there, the fire will just get bigger. And bigger . . . until the whole eight-foot-tall and five-foot-wide shack is engulfed in flames and people in the dorms across the way pull those fire alarms and fire trucks come and you have to keep apologizing and then finally run when the campus police get there. They're called jumping jacks, these things. They're, like, only fifty cents a pack.

#2

Look at all of these smug people with air-conditioning in their cars passing me on Interstate 10. Look at them . . . knowing nothing about pouring water over yourself and keeping the windows down and putting ice from the Circle K Store in your lap. Knowing nothing about finding shade to sleep in by two-thirty in the afternoon and starting out again around nine or ten at night when the sun is gone. Don't they realize that they can just sleep in college campus theaters and libraries when it gets too hot? It amazes me how stupid so many people can be. Stupid people with, uh, air-conditioning.

#3

At around midnight, looked up and saw a coyote at the side of the highway and right at the edge of the head-lights, and there are these incredibly tall things in the bluish white light that I realize are cactus. Must be in the desert now and far from Los Angeles and even far from Palm Springs and all that. Finally escaped anything that might be following me. Finally free from things that haven't worked out up until now. The windows are down and I hear the Doppler effect of driving past distant coy-ote howls, and for once in my life I feel like I'm too fast to catch. Dashboard lights reflecting off the windshield. No stores, no other cars, no towns that I can see. Gas gauge is like a little northern star and you can see the needle fallen down past the letter E reflecting off the—

Oh, shit.

I am an idiot.

7

Past the Crab Pot

and Just Before the
Merry-Go-Round

By the time I got to Seattle, I was a year and a half late. Turns out, by the time something is on the cover of national magazines, the explosion part has pretty much already happened. I could feel there was an explosion, just as the magazine had said. I could tell that if you were here at the right time, you would have already gone on your way. You would be in a van or on a bus or in a plane reading about your album selling more than you thought possible as each day passed. Since I was sort of too late to be picked for a team, I had to change my stance. Enter the "Alternative rock sold out and I'm not going to" phase.

Ah, yes. Brilliant.

Weeks before I would arrive too late in Seattle, there was a man already in Seattle who had come most recently from Hawaii, where he managed a large chain of bars and "eateries." And when he arrived, he, too, had a plan to become something large and different . . . something reinvented. Soon he would no longer be just the burned-out manager of a large chain of restaurants in his early forties who—despite a decent gut from having the best steaks for every one of his employee meals washed down with top-shelf cognacs and a Baileys milk shake for dessert—could still get "the prime night-shift waitress tail."

As I lurched north on Interstate 5, only recently recovered from mishaps in Austin, he was already in place. Fate was already in motion. Soon I would find this man. He was already well on his way to becoming something different from what he was. He was, in fact, already well on his way to becoming the king of espresso coffee drinks, ice cream, and coffee-related apparel and gift items. And so, by economy coach class and economy car, we both crawled north and northwest to our Lourdes to be rid of whatever had made mutants of us. Because certainly and somehow there was a way for the world's most downtrodden and isolated to be the center of attention in Seattle. I myself had seen the proof of this divine intervention in an apparition on the cover of a music magazine while still in Texas.

Maybe two weeks before I pulled into town and started sleeping on a remote acquaintance's couch, this man walked—or maybe drove his newly leased late-model Ford Ranger pickup truck with optional sport package (stripe, chrome wheels, tinted windows)—to the newspaper office to place a classified advertisement. After I had moved my body from the sleeping position and into the sitting position on said remote acquaintance's couch, I picked up the newspaper and saw the ad he had placed. It said that there were two jobs open at an espresso café. His espresso café. This is what he was starting after years of managing corporate-owned resorts, bars, and, most recently, theme restaurants in Hawaii. His transformation had already started, and now that he was ready to hire his first employees, my transformation was about to begin. The ad said that one position was for a counterperson, but there was also a position for . . . a manager.

Ahhhhh, counterperson, I thought to myself.

This was something I could most likely do. How difficult could it be? You stand. That's probably the hardest part. Past that, you work the espresso machine thing, ask people what you can get for them, develop a few catchphrases to use to thank them, and point them to the condiments. You probably do it all in a slightly different order than that, but you get the point. I had seen these people. Sort of leftist, vaguely well-traveled underachievers with a neo-hippie influence and a solid catalog of seventies pop culture references. Let's face it: They're somehow cooler than you even though they're getting your coffee. They always know the names of stuff that you can't pronounce, and they seem to know a lot about other types of government ("fascist!"), and this would be a chance for me to grow. The job would make me cooler and no longer quite the misfit. Instead I would seem like a misfit by choice, plus somehow smarter than you about government and art and things like that. So I was up for this. Maybe even thinking I could be the best counterperson somehow. Learn all the drinks, learn how to talk about some guy named Noam Chomsky and about socialism or . . . uh, whatever. And independent films and alternative rock. This, actually, could be where I kind of get my start. Maybe once I made it as a famous pop culture icon of some sort, my most knowledgeable fans would say, "Yeah, we used to go to the café in Seattle whenever he was working. It was great. When we saw him [In concert? At his book signing? In that new movie? On *Saturday Night Live*?] last week, we remembered how great it was when he used to work right down the street."

I'm not much of a leftist. I'm more of a "Hang a left at the mall and it's the second apartment complex on your right," but I pulled together a little something of an outfit that I thought was right for the part.

- Tan jeans with an off-brand surf company logo on the back pocket (Surf = Nonconformist)
- Off-brand hiking boots (Hiking = Screw society's rules)
- Brown wool socks (Wool = Screw society's rules?)
- Plain gray T-shirt (This doesn't really equal anything, which is pretty cool. You know, cool that I don't care that it equals nothing in terms of a statement. P.S. Screw society's rules.)

I clipped out the ad and started to head downtown to figure out where this café was. I got downtown and asked a few people where 1388 Alaskan Way was. It was down a lot of stairs. Then, down a narrow alley, and then across a big main street, and then I was there. Why is it here? This is not cool, this area.

This is the waterfront. This is probably the least cool area of almost any city by the water. There are tourists here. There are mimes here. There is cotton candy, caramel apples, little souvenir killer whales and space needles, merry-go-rounds, outdoor puppet shows about the earliest settlers of the Pacific Northwest, a restaurant called the Crab Pot, a man who looks like a former community college professor with a mildly methadone-laced stare who has a parrot that will sit on your shoulder for a photo, a shop that sells T-shirts with your picture on the front, and . . . Smitty's Espresso.

Located just past the Crab Pot and just before the merry-go-round, right across from the shop that sells sweatshirts and T-shirts. It is not cool. It is not leftist. It is not the center of Seattle counterculture. It is clean. It is brightly lit. It serves ice cream and espresso and sells red short-sleeve polyester and cotton-knit sport shirts with the Smitty's Espresso logo embroidered on the breast pocket. It is presumed that you, the customer, will want to purchase one of these shirts when you see me, the employee, wearing one as part of my uniform.

Yes, there will be a uniform.

JEANS

Must be crisply pressed, new, dark denim. Employees are responsible for making sure jeans are in presentable shape as outlined herein.

SHOES

White, and only white, athletic shoes in new condition. No scuffs. No graffiti along edges of shoe. No large multicolor logos.

STAFF SHIRT

You're given one on a sign-out basis, and may purchase additional shirts with an employee discount if keeping one in clean order is not within your daily means.

Note: Employees will be sent home at manager's discretion if uniforms are not up to the standards described above.

Yes, there will be a manual to read, which has been printed out on the owner's home computer. Yes, there will be surprise tests on milk pitcher maintenance, spoon placement, steam wand cleanliness, and proper uniform dress code. Yes, these tests can occur while you're helping customers. Doesn't that make you want to focus on, study and retain, and then properly display your knowledge of this material? It should. Think about it. You will be in front of customers—maybe even a bit overwhelmed by the number of customers that tends to result from high-traffic tourist retail venues like the waterfront—and afraid of families and of the voice in your head that has told you to work here now in this uniform for this strange and short man who yells maniacally about how he will someday be the McDonald's of coffee drinks, ice cream, and coffee-related apparel and gift items. You'll know it's a surprise test

because the little office door will swing open, and there will
be a pause. A pause in which you feel like you're waiting to
see if the groundhog will come out of its hole and see its
shadow. With a slightly different pause each time, he will
eventually appear. Sometimes delayed for only the couple
of seconds it takes to put out his cigarette, and sometimes
a bit longer, if, say, he has to put out his cigarette and turn
off his adding machine. After appearing in the doorway, he
will then march toward you in a large red short-sleeve
poly/cotton-knit sport shirt that is filled out a little differ-
ently in the stomach and waist area than your medium red
short-sleeve knit sport shirt. He will wear that pressured
little grin that is supposed to convey good cheer, but when
mixed with his trademark stress and almost amphetamine
congeniality, looks more like a sitcom version of Jack
Nicholson in *The Shining*. It looks like the grin of a confused jackal or pestered coyote, or of an uncle resentfully
attending a family cookout that took him away from a
horse race or a hooker, but since nobody in the family
really knows about the horse races or hookers, he just sits
there with the consolation prize of Coors beer and ham-
burgers, acting happy to see you . . . that kind of grin. And
he will grade you poorly in front of two customers when
you use your "spoon hand" instead of your "steam pitcher
hand" to reach for the pitcher of steamed milk. You will,
for some reason, daydream of your role being played by
Scott Baio in the bad television movie-of-the-week version
of all of this. And the strangest aspect of everything happening here—the part you are confused most by—is that
this man (who has just slapped your spoon hand as you
lost points on the test) is a good five inches shorter than

you, which makes it start to feel like one of those horror movies you and your sister used to see advertised on movie posters at the cinema in the mall, in which a small doll, child, or ventriloquist's dummy is capable of frightening grown adults, even though it is a fraction of their size and permanently smiling. Now you understand how the tiny doll was able to frighten them all. And then you'll actually entertain the nightmare of Papa, as he is wont to call himself during the surprise tests, having actually fathered you, as his self-imposed nickname implies. Jesus. Just think. What if? But I'm getting way ahead of myself here, so let's back up. Let's get back to the facts about how all of this came to be.

Yes, there was a job interview.

Yes, it was explained, much to my disbelief, that I was the sole candidate for manager.

Yes, it was explained to me that there would be an opportunity for me to buy a franchise and for the first time in my life actually *own* a business instead of working for someone else. Perfect. Finally, things would be different for me. I would be an owner . . . eventually. But first I would learn the ropes by working for Mr. Smith.

ALSO:

Yes, my idea of flirting with the most gorgeous waitress from the Crab Pot, who was my age and so, so, so beautiful and cool, was to give her extra proofs-of-purchase on her Smitty's Espresso punch card, so that she would be seven-tenths of the way to a free coffee drink of her choice after having purchased only *one* instead of seven.

And yes, I was the sole employee, and so all of those

so-called rules, regulations, tests, manuals, and policies for "all employees" applied only to me . . . but that would all change. Mr. Smith's sister was in Hawaii planning to undertake the same personal journey of transformation he did months ago: quitting her job at a chain restaurant and moving to Seattle to work on the waterfront for her brother.

"You're going to *love* Tammy. Very similar personalities. You two are going to get along *great!*" The groundhog beamed.

This vexed me. What personality had I even remotely displayed? It had been a month and I'd felt paralyzed with fear and disbelief the entire time. But maybe I was sort of starting to develop and showcase a little bit of a personality . . . the personality of . . . an eventual franchise owner? I mean, I was getting decent scores on my surprise uniform checks—I hadn't been sent home once. Aside from my problem delegating the proper drink-making task to the assigned hand, I wasn't doing so badly when I stopped to think about it. Maybe this had been like the army for me. You know, maybe I was finally growing up and taking on the responsibilities of showing up and serving people's needs. I mean, let's face it . . . I AM THE MANAGER OF THE WHOLE DAMN SHOP AND I WILL EVENTUALLY OWN ONE OF THESE. I was the man making the drinks, doing the books, dipping the ice cream while not forgetting to wear my state-mandated athletic wrist-support mechanism, locking the place up, and cleaning the place down. Maybe *that's* what he meant by personality! Maybe things *were* starting to happen for me.

I was feeling pretty good about everything. My ideas were even being listened to by Mr. Smith.

"You know, we could pour a shot of espresso over a scoop of ice cream and have a whole new item on our hands here," I casually mentioned while adjusting the Velcro on my wrist guard before scooping out some chocolate (single; cup, not cone) ice cream for a customer.

"Not a bad idea!" He beamed and then explained to the customer, "I gotta watch this guy, he's after my job! He won't stop until he owns his own Smitty's franchise! You know, that's the problem with running a working model of an affordable coffee drink franchise—anyone who's a hard worker and would like to own a franchise for little money down is going to be working for themselves, not me, thanks to Smitty's Espresso."

The customer seemed uninterested in anything but the ice cream she had ordered and that I was taking too long to serve. She seemed even less interested the more Smith enthused about his shop and what a wonderful day it would be when every neighborhood in America had one of his shops in it. She rolled her eyes one final time and walked away.

Who the hell cared? These were the kinds of ideas I was capable of having with my new eventual-owner personality, and these were the crazy days when anything still seemed possible for Mr. Smith and all employees (me). The sky was the limit. And then Tammy showed up.

She arrived the very next day and I noticed right away something was changing. And one day the door to the little office swung open. Tammy came out, not yet having stubbed out her Benson & Hedges Menthol 100, still drinking coffee from her super-large gas station refillable commuter mug, and saying that the big guy wanted to see me. I took off my wrist-support mechanism and put the scoop back into its small tub of forty-five-degree water (filled a quarter of an inch from the top), which was to be rinsed and refreshed at noon, two-thirty, and four o'clock. I stepped into the tiny office.

"Well, I bet you're glad Tammy's here," he said.

"Where? Oh. Yes."

What happened next happened in a very quick whirlwind of details, most of which aren't important. To get the full effect of the whirlwind of details, simply imagine a regular-sized man telling you everything about coffee, coffee businesses, franchises, the importance of family, and goals all at once—all in about three seconds—and then suddenly shrinking down to take on the form of the evil ventriloquist's doll and doing his little murderer doll grin as he lands on the phrase, "And you will be the manager of the coffee cart out front on the street!"

No.

And that is the way that I found myself quite literally out on the street. It felt like being ousted from your own dream company by the board of directors. And, of course, this meant new rules.

NOTICE TO ALL STREET CART EMPLOYEES

Uniforms can be altered when working a cart shift. WHITE long-sleeve turtleneck shirt (or blouse) can be worn UNDER your red staff shirt.

*All employees can also wear a BLUE jacket.
Jacket should be unzipped to show company
colors of shirt. When summer arrives, cart employees may wear hemmed BLUE shorts. Man-
agement must "approve" all jackets and shorts.
See before buying.*

The misplaced quotation marks took the brunt of
my rage. "Approve." Oh, you "fucker," Mr. Smith. You're
edging me "out," aren't "you"?

In the mornings, I would push the cart along the
empty waterfront pier while happy carousel music played
from brittle speakers, even though the place was deathly
still and empty, and everything made it seem like a
haunted harbor in an episode of *Scooby-Doo.* Somewhere
an unshaven crook hoisted cargo from a ship using a net
with a squeaky rope-and-pulley mechanism. Somewhere
in a van there was a dog that could sort of talk. And there
I was, in my big, dumb uniform, pushing a big, dumb
coffee-vending street cart right past all of it and along
the waterfront until I arrived at the X that the ground-
hog/jackal/evil doll had painted on the sidewalk, to mark
the spot where the cart should come to rest and have its
wheels locked into place. The first thing I would do after
locking the wheels in place was plug the line into the elec-
trical outlet and crank out the cart's blue-and-white-
striped awning.

It would be about 7:30 A.M. by that point and I
would switch on the cart's tiny espresso machine. All-
systems-go time. And there I was, setting up shop in my
approved cold-weather outdoor uniform, the freeway

above me crammed with noisy early-morning commuters, the street and sidewalk in front of me barren, since locals loathed the waterfront and tourists wouldn't arrive for another two months at least. And I would basically just sit in the canvas director's chair that was provided and wonder what the hell my life was going to turn into. One or two customers was about the peak, but the gambling uncle–like boss man didn't seem to mind.

"Oh, they'll come soon enough. Just get the hang of running everything. They're on their way from all over the country."

My one or two customers were usually people my age who had gigs inside the shops or restaurants along the waterfront and who took pity on me. Dave, a waiter at the Crab Pot, was always good for dropping by and buying a cup of coffee. He seemed like a happy guy. He would always know how much money he made the day before in tips. It was always way more than I made, and I knew that anywhere between one and five dollars of it was mine, depending on how many drinks I had snuck over on my shift the day prior. I was always drowning my sorrows about clearly now being out of the running as an eventual franchise owner by sneaking drinks at the Crab Pot and shots of espresso from the cart. Sometimes I would have stolen a cigarette from Mr. Smith or Tammy to enjoy with my coffee.

THE CRAB POT SPEEDBALL

You'll need:

Two shots of off-brand whiskey
One shot of espresso (no whipped cream)

Before removing the cash from the cart's till (security measure), draw one shot of espresso and leave it to cool. Walk quickly to the Crab Pot. Sit at the bar and order a double shot of the most affordable whiskey, drink quickly, and return to cart. Load cash bank back into register till. Close register, drink espresso shot quickly. Sit back in canvas chair and wait for the caffeine and grain alcohol to work in concert with each other.

CAFÉ CRÈME DE MENTHOL

You'll need:

One shot of espresso with whipped cream
One Benson & Hedges Menthol 100 cigarette

Top shot of espresso with dollop of whipped cream topping, ignite cigarette, and sit out of (potential) customer's view, behind cart near left or right back wheel. Drink espresso in one quick shot, whipped cream and all. As you bend down to put whipped cream topping back into fridge, reach down next to cart's wheel, pick up ignited cigarette, and inhale.

Sitting outside, it felt like I was the kid kicked out of class for saying the wrong thing at the wrong time. And my mornings were spent sitting under the cart's colorful awning in my canvas director's chair, sneaking free shots of espresso and ducking down behind the cart occasionally to suck the nitrous oxide propellant from the whipped cream cans in the fridge and then holding my breath to get the nitrous buzz as I took my seat again, watching all of the early-morning freeway traffic pass by overhead.

CAFÉ N₂O (SOMETIMES CALLED "MR. BRAIN" OR "THE ELECTRIC SLIDE")

Same as the Café Crème de Menthol, except that the nitrous oxide propellant in the whipped-cream can is substituted as the inhalant.

Set can of whipped cream out of (potential) customer's view behind cart near left or right back wheel. Drink espresso in one quick shot. Act like you dropped something. Bend down out of view to "pick up what you dropped," reach for can stashed next to cart's wheel, pick up and inhale. Hold breath, return to "at ease" position behind cart, and enjoy.

There I was high on nitrous and hoping nobody ordered whipped cream on their mocha. I hoped that's what the boss meant by "getting the hang of running everything." The whipped-cream-can nitrous hits wore off slowly if I didn't breathe while watching the freeway overhead. Every car piloted by somebody who had somewhere to go and a reason to get there. Every single one of them heading in the right direction, and up on an overpass about two stories too high to stop and buy a cup of coffee from the likes of me down here on the street. When the whoosh of the freeway traffic started sounding like a big electronic metallic monster, it was time to exhale the nitrous so that I didn't pass out in my director's chair, to be found unconscious and drooling on my stupid uniform. As the days and traffic went by and by and by and byeeeerrrreeeeereeeeeep (exhale), I started to enjoy sitting in my canvas director's chair. I hated my job, but I loved the way I felt in that chair. Like some kind of movie star or something, or some big Hollywood director. (Cue freeway traffic! Good,

good . . . okay, slow it down a little bit, we need to see the
drivers . . . good . . . nice . . . keep them coming. Cut! Perfect! Print that and let's move on, people.) And almost on
perfect cue, as if by sitting in a director's chair day after
day getting high on espresso, canned dessert topping, and
Crab Pot drink specials, a woman appeared almost out of
nowhere and informed me that she was the locations manager for a movie that was filming in town. She asked if I
could cater espresso drinks to the set for a fee. I said no.
She asked again. I said no again. She again stated that it
would be a great way to make some extra money. I once
again said no. Jesus, do I look like a caterer? I wondered.
Ah, and then I realized what was happening here. I told
her that I wanted to be in the movie she was working on
and that, while I didn't do catering, I knew of people who
did and could get their phone numbers. She said she'd
make me a deal that if I called her with the phone numbers
that would get her out of her espresso catering bind, she
would give me the phone number of the woman doing the
local casting on this film. And I came through, and she did,
too. Phone numbers were traded and I called the local casting woman. She asked if I could meet her at the Embassy
Suites hotel in the suburbs of Seattle, about forty minutes
outside the city. I had the next day off and took a cab with
the forty dollars that I practically tricked the ATM into
giving me from my checking account (cab ended up being,
like, thirty-eight with tip!) to meet her in the lobby, and
she walked me back to a room where they were doing the
casting. She and her business partner sat in a huge suite
filled with photos of actors and résumés and Polaroid pic-

tures of wardrobes. They took one look at me and said, "College buddy number two buying sunglasses!" and asked me if I could commit to shooting this movie for ten or fifteen days. I excused myself for a moment to use the pay phone in the lobby. I knew the call to Mr. Smith would be a tense one, as the big Seattle boat fair at the waterfront would be happening while I was using my vacation days to make my Hollywood debut.

Bad Hollywood adaptation version of conversation:

INT. HOTEL LOBBY—DAY.

> ### EMPLOYEE GUY
> (Into phone)
>
>> Look, I can't explain it right now, but I've basically just been offered a part in a Hollywood feature film, man. And let's face it, you don't need me to make this happen. Not now that you have Tammy here. Listen to me! You ... two ... are going to do great, man. Just let it be the way it's supposed to be, you know? (Pause) We couldn't have planned any of this.

> CUT TO:

INT. ESPRESSO SHOP—SAME.

BOSS/OWNER is on the phone. On his desk we see the employee schedule for the next week.

> ### BOSS/OWNER
>
>> No ... wrong. You listen to me: Do the right thing. Hollywood is going to chew

you up and spit you out. You don't have
the guts for it! That is, not yet. If you
come back here and give this everything
you've got, you'll eventually leave here
with the guts you need to *own* Hollywood.
Now, what's it gonna be?

                              CUT BACK TO:
INT. HOTEL LOBBY—DAY.

We see EMPLOYEE GUY hang up the phone and
walk away. As the phone is slammed down, current
Top 40 radio single starts playing in soundtrack.

The actual conversation that day went more like
this:

"Um, I can't work next week . . . plus the following
week. I need to use my vacation time."

"Who is this?"

"Dan."

"Are you quitting? Because you need to be here both
of those weeks."

"Uh, well . . . I guess so, then. Because I have an
opportunity to—"

"Fine. Turn your uniforms in."

And with that I was officially working on a movie
and officially fired/quit the espresso business in a matter
of a week or so. He had come by plane, and I had come by
car, and looking back, I can see that as much as I disliked
him as an employer, we had a lot in common in that we
were looking for very similar epic lives in our own individual ways. I was glad that I was moving on and that the
meeting with the casting director had gone so well. The

only awkward part of the meeting with the casting people, really, was standing in front of the hotel afterward, with my back to the big windows of their first-floor suite/office, as I waited for a bus that would take me all the way back into the city on my last two dollars. In the maze of the landscaped metro business park where the Embassy Suites hotel is located, the buses only come every couple of hours . . . so you just kind of end up standing there at the bus stop on the crisp white sidewalk next to the bright green grass. I was hoping they wouldn't look out the window for the next couple of hours and see me standing there like an overgrown schoolkid who was held back thirteen grades. I'm sure every up-and-coming movie star has felt like that at one time or another, though.

OPEN LETTER TO
THE KING OF COFFEE

Dear Mr. Smith,

It was so, so, so long ago and I'm sure you barely remember. I should remind you of who I am: Sole employee of your business in very beginning, and then I was put outside (no big deal) to run the curbside espresso cart when Tammy (nothing against her) came into the picture. There are a handful of things I could admit in hopes of clearing my conscience here (tended to drink at the Crab Pot and then afterward steal those horrible long, thin menthol cigarettes from you and your sister when you two weren't looking, so I could take them out to the cart and maintain my Crab Pot lunch break buzz by smoking your family's cigarettes and inhaling the propellant from the whipped cream cans in the espresso cart's little fridge. I always called that little fridge the minibar). But to be honest, I feel like we're pretty even on everything. You had to know there would be some repercussions after kicking me out to the (admit it, less favorable) curbside coffee cart. You had to take care of your sister first, which is exactly what I would've done in your shoes. I do have to apologize for quitting on you the week before the big weekend boat fair crowd. Well, I had a chance to be in a Hollywood movie! At least it rained and your crowd was small and manageable. You were right that I wouldn't become a movie star by appearing in *The Vanishing* as "College guy #2 buying sunglasses." I remember telling you that I *knew* it wouldn't make me a movie star, but in all honesty I was faking the level-headed attitude and was a little surprised to find that it didn't make me a movie star. Anyway, you ended up being right about me going broke after the movie left town, but I eventually learned to bartend (free drinks and no more having to steal cigarettes from folks like you and Tammy!), and had a decent time of it. I've had a handful of ups and down with endeavors (see surrounding chapters in book).

I heard through the grapevine shortly after quitting that the employee you hired to replace me was a small, wiry Puerto Rican kid who wore three pagers and a red bandanna (did whole uniform rule go to hell after I left?) while he worked, and that the cash register count was always short at the end of the day if he was working. It's the only time in my life I've felt like I may have been a better employee than my replacement—although maybe you figured that he stole less from the till than what you were spending in whipped cream and extra menthols with me around (joking).

Well, I hope that you're well, and no hard feelings here, just for the record.

Best,
Dan Kennedy

FAILING TO MAKE SMALL TALK WITH THE OCCASIONAL ESPRESSO CART CUSTOMER

Customer #1: Guy Wearing T-Shirt That Has Ghostly Pictures of Gang Members on It and Says Rest in Peace

ME: Hey, they finally get some peace now, right? They deserve some peace.

HIM: *[Looking down at shirt and then up at me]* That's cold, bro.

ME: No, I just mean . . . they maybe . . . got hassled too much, you know. . . .

HIM: Don't mean they wanna be dead.

ME: Oh, no. No, not at all. That's not what I mean. Don't kill somebody just because their life is hard.

HIM: They pay you enough to work out here, bro?

ME: I guess. I don't know, yeah.

HIM: You don't wanna make more out here?

ME: Not really. I mean, I'm already out here eight hours a day.

HIM: But you know what I'm sayin'? You wanna make more out here?

ME: Right. More dough. Well . . . no, because . . . I'm already out here? From eight to four?

HIM: *[Smiling and leaving]* Take care of yourself, bro.

ME: Okay. Have a good one.

Customer #2: A State Ferry Employee in Eddie Bauer Jacket

HER: Hi. Can I get a double tall mocha?

[I start making it.]

HER: Are you keeping warm out here? I guess you can have all the free coffee you want, right?

ME: Thanks.

HER:

ME: Okay, three sixty-five.

HER: There you go. Where's your tip jar?

ME: Oh, uh . . . should be on your side of the espresso machine there.

HER: *[Looking down]* Where?

Customer #3: Beautiful Waitress from Waterfront Restaurant

ME: Hi, how are you? Good to see you. Okaaay. Let's see here . . .

HER: Can I get a tall latté?

ME: Yeah. Yeah, no problem. Sure. Okay. Let's see here . . .

[I start making it. Drop the cup. Nervous . . . No big deal, though, I just get a new one.]

HER: You're a friend of Dave's, right?

ME: Oh . . . yeah . . . yeah, great guy.

HER: He's funny.

ME: Really funny guy. He's the one guy who can make you laugh no matter what kind of mood you're in, you know? Funny. Really cracks me up. Not, like, the annoying kind of funny. He's, like, "smart funny." Yeah . . . love seeing Dave. Great guy. Dave's funny.

[Trying to think of something else I can say to her so I don't keep talking about the only mutual friend we have.]

ME: Yep . . . you gotta love Dave.

[Still trying to think of something to say to her.]
[She pays and is getting ready to leave. I'm kind of looking down at my shoes, still trying to think of something to say to her. You can tell it's killing me.]

HER: He's, um . . . working tonight . . . if you really want to see him.

Customer #4: A Waterfront Security Guy

[I'm ducking down behind cart, accessing whipped cream cans in fridge.]

HIM: Anybody home back there?

[I get up, seeing that I have a customer. I prep the espresso machine to make drink.]

HIM: I'll take one of your café mochas.

[I start making it.]

HIM: Nice day out here.

[I nod in agreement.]

HIM: Business picking up?

[I shrug my shoulders and make the "so-so" sign by wobbling my hand back and forth.]

HIM: It'll get busier in a month or two.

[He starts to hand me money, but I make a "don't worry about it" gesture, since it's policy to give the security guys a free drink at the cart.]

HIM: Can I push my luck and get some whipped cream on there?

[I grab a can from the fridge, turn it upside down, and depress the nozzle, but the cream comes out like thick milk instead of fluffed-up whipped cream.]

HIM: Woops, that one's lookin' pretty empty.

ME: *[Huge exhale]* Some . . . of . . . these . . . cans . . . kind of go flat.

8

It's Not Saturday Night

(and This Is Not Live)

Being in the movie business is a lot like spending eleven days in front of a minimart, waiting to appear on camera for around two to six seconds, during which time I'd buy sunglasses inside of a gas station minimart while not saying a word or looking at the camera. And at the end of each day I would get a ride home from European Backpacker #1 and Male Twins in Store, and comfort myself in knowing that I had made $125.

Money. Oh, sweet money, I thought to myself on the way home.

Money, oh, come to me, sweet cash money, I continued to think for two months after my last day on this movie, which is how long it took to get the money.

I spent my downtime rationing stale cigarettes and freeze-dried noodle soups, like a hardened G.I., or a film noir fugitive, or a . . . uh, well . . . movie extra who was broke and now without work. After thirty days, something occurred to me: Be a movie extra again. And I called European Backpacker #1, who told me that there was some work in town on a movie called *Sleepless in Seattle*. And so I called the casting director. This time when we met, she sized me up and exclaimed, "Dinner Eater in the restaurant scene!" (Going through my head at that moment: Please let them use real food in the scene. Food that can be eaten.) But as fate would have it, my character was just a single yuppie guy having a cocktail. And so there I was sitting for an eternity in a trendy restaurant wearing a suit I could never afford and drinking a prop glass of murky, warm olive water (martini) while Tom Hanks took an urgent phone call about thirty-five feet away . . . again and again and again, until he took the urgent phone call in exactly the way the director wanted him to.

THINKING WHILE SIPPING A FAKE MARTINI IN THE BACKGROUND

- I could do this for real. I mean, actually be this guy. The suit, the job, the trendy alcoholic beverages after work at a restaurant like this. If I could just turn this fake version into a real version, I would have this life.

- Certainly by now Nora Ephron has noticed the semi-attractive young man sipping the fake martini *perfectly* in every single take.
- My God, Tom Hanks. How hard is it to answer a goddamn phone? Let's do this.
- Somewhere there's a factory where olives like this one are stuffed with pimiento and then jammed into jars. All of it is done by machine, I bet. It is completely by chance that this particular olive should wind up here in front of these lights and cameras. This olive had no idea it would end up in a movie and in thousands of theaters. Poor olive, too dumb to even know how lucky it is to have ended up here. Or worse, delusional enough to think that this somehow makes it a special olive. Oh, you are just a little olive in the background, so calm down.
- What if I am so good at being a movie extra that I actually get lost in my character for years at a time without knowing it, like some insane genius actor?
- Is there ice cream left in my freezer or did I come home drunk and eat it?
- What seems to be the problem, Tom Hanks? Jesus. This suit is itching.
- I should be a movie actor.

And after *Sleepless in Seattle*, there was a cable TV movie called *Better Off Dead*. They were dealing with a shortage of male extras on their weekday shoot, and I was relied upon to be a drunk patron in a strip club in one scene, a court bailiff in the next scene, and a newspaper reporter on the court steps in yet another scene. I had never felt so successful and confident. There I stood, a man in uniform next to the judge with my thumbs tucked behind my belt buckle, seeming to say, "Yes, I know you have seen me drunk and leering at strippers, but I have gotten my act together. I have been a member of the Associated Press, for instance. And now I'm here today starting my career in the justice system, the very system that would've sentenced me back in my drunk-and-leering-at-strippers phase on Tuesday." But it wasn't long before the fifteen-hour days and huge career changes took their toll. I burned out. I needed to stop. Stop this insane Hollywood (Seattle) roller coaster of a life where all that matters is being a star (extra) and nothing is real anymore.

And after my latest Hollywood movie money ($718) was gone, I was aimless and broke again, and unable to get my job back at the espresso cart. I auditioned for a small independent film and was required to read a monologue. I read something about rationing stale cigarettes and freeze-dried noodle soups. As I was leaving the audition, sure that I hadn't gotten the part, the director called my name before I got to the door. I turned around with a smile and told him that I was certain that I hadn't gotten the part, and couldn't believe this was happening. He said I was right, that I hadn't gotten the part, and then further clarified that nothing, in fact, was happening. He just wanted to know if I had written the monologue that I read. I said yes. He said he really thought it was "great—kind of depressing, but you really nailed the writing."

Shut up. Whatever.

I spent my days rationing stale cigarettes and freeze-dried noodle soups again. And again, after a while, something occurred to me: That director said he thought my writing was great, and depressing. I should . . . be a writer on . . . a comedy show! Yes, yes . . . *Saturday . . . Night . . . Live*. Obvious! Face it! It's been my dream ever since I was allowed to stay up and watch it in the sixth grade! This is it!

Suddenly my life seemed to make sense:

1. Voted "Best Personality" in fifth and sixth grades.
2. Suspended for biting satirical essay of seventh-grade homeroom teacher, who was considered by most of the student body to be not unlike a chronic hypochondriac type who killed time by peeking in neighbors' windows and setting small piles of dried grass and leaves on fire.
3. Currently living on diet of stale tobacco and freeze-dried noodles, sodium, and water.

I was done with being a small-time guy. I would go to New York and make this happen. This time it would be the real thing . . . the big time. I counted up the money I had and added it to the paychecks that would still be processed over the next two months: two hundred and sixty-something dollars, with a possible extra twenty-something dollars that I seemed to have mislaid or left in other pants.

So, maybe almost three hundred.

Okay, new plan: I wouldn't move to New York.

Besides, I didn't even need to. Because just as there
are television networks in New York, there are also these
little television stations (just as good) called network affiliates in smaller markets (like Seattle). And these network
affiliates produce local programming (just as good as
national programming), maybe a show about local arts
and entertainment, and maybe that's kind of their local
version of (and just as good as) a big network entertainment magazine show like *Entertainment Tonight*. Or maybe
there's a comedy show . . . a comedy show that is sort
of the network affiliate's version of *Saturday Night Live*.
Maybe it's called, like, *Big Crazy Night Live* or something
along those lines. Maybe, almost like the show in New York
that it is arguably modeled after, the comedy sketches are
mixed in with musical guests. And maybe a spoof of the
local news in which the fake anchorman would be saying
things, and the small studio audience would be laughing,
and there would almost be a little slice of New York or
Los Angeles alive and well in a small television studio out
near the lake, just past the Burger King where I would go
once my movie paychecks arrived. Sitting at Burger King
one night, I realized that I would be a television writer
right here in Seattle without having to go to New York
(plus: broke). I think that if you could have seen me sitting at that Burger King finishing the last of my fries and
staring at apparently nothing but the air in front of my
face, you would have thought to yourself: Look at that
professional television comedy writer sitting right here at
Burger King in Seattle.

Instead of the rationing and waiting, I spent my
days opening my eyes to everything that was happening

around me and wondering what comedic material might lie in the seemingly mundane occurrences. And so, regarding the fast-food restaurant called Dick's: Are there in fact employees who act like complete dicks? No, not this time. Maybe I should go back tomorrow? Okay, not that time, either, really. And not the next time, either, or the time after that. The only thing funny or pathetic about this fast-food restaurant was the guy in the corner who had gained a noticeable ten pounds in the course of a month's worth of daily visits. Yeah, the regular there in the booth who appeared to be straining to hear every word each cashier said to each customer. Yeah. Fatty . . . the guy with the notepad and little tape recorder.

I hung around in Pike Place Public Market watching tourists from around the world walk by. When anybody even remotely Japanese passed by, I came out of the shadows and followed them, because a guy in the cast of the show could play Japanese perfectly. What were they doing? Anything funny? What were they saying? What did I imagine they were saying? ("Ass, assy, ass, ass, assy, see slippery me.") Hey, was that funny? By the time I snuck up on my third family, I realized that security was watching me. Me, the guy who stood behind posts until he could sneak into a passing Asian family and walk with them until they got too suspicious. I would learn approximately ten years later that all of this is the exact opposite of what seems to work when one is looking for material to write about.

After not finding a comedy sketch in the local fast-food restaurant, the local public market, the local office supply store, or the local police officers (the show already had a police officer sketch), I eventually managed to think up some scripts and local news items and fax them in. And after faxing them in from the stationery store down the street from the mother-in-law cottage I was sharing with Dave, my friend from the Crab Pot, I came home and found that there was a message on the answering machine. It was the producer of the show, saying that he had taken a look at my material and would like to set up a time to talk.

I wanted to take a moment to think about what I would say on the phone call, and so I retired to doing what Dave and I did whenever we had something we needed to think about or figure out: I stood in the yard of the little mother-in-law cottage (backyard of regular-person home that the cottage was located behind) and threw apples and rocks at the tree trunk by the front walkway and launched a few bottle rockets into the park that bordered our rented cottage. I stood pensively throwing the tiny crab apples against the tree that bore them—occasionally using one of the pieces of broken apple as a bottle rocket launch pad—while the children in the normal-person home looked down from their second-story bedroom window, wondering, without making a sound, if this was what it was like to be twenty-five. I felt happy to be able to provide them with at least a more interesting example of that than did the other men my age, who were driving sensible cars to mid-level jobs after (not only getting accepted to but also finishing) college. An example in which rocks and apples were tossed at tree trunks, and imaginary park targets were subject to air attack, and where professional television comedy-writing jobs were there for the taking. I returned the producer's call, and was high on the fact that I had arrived at a point in my life where I could use a phrase like, "I returned the producer's call." For the four business days that stood between me and my appointment (professional television comedy-writing interview), it was a phrase I worked into almost all of my conversations around the house.

For instance, Dave might have said, "Hey, do you want to go get a beer?"

And I might have replied, "Let's see, I returned the producer's call about my writing samples, so . . . sure, Dave. Let's grab a beer."

Or if Dave said something like, "Hey, I'm taking my rent check over, do you want me to take yours?" I might have said, "Thanks . . . that would be great. Actually . . . I returned the producer's call about my writing samples, so I'll just walk over with you."

"You did that two days ago."

"Did what two days ago?"

"Returned that call."

"Oh, the producer's call? About my writing samples? Yeah, it's all taken care of."

My spirits were high. I was joking around more. Playing more practical jokes around the house. Like the one where you're still lying in bed and you hear your roommate and you start thinking of a way to startle him because you know he thinks you're already up and out of the house for the day. One morning, Dave was downstairs in the kitchen doing dishes, and I was upstairs (wood lad-

der that leads through crawl-space hole in ceiling and into
my bedroom area), and the plan I was lying there thinking about goes like this:

- Dave thinks I'm already gone. He doesn't realize
  that I've slept late and I'm still in my bed upstairs
  directly above the kitchen.
- I will quietly prop open my huge bedroom window,
  which is right against the side of my bed, and
  directly above the kitchen window. Then I will
  quietly inch out from under my covers on my
  stomach and backward, pushing my legs out the
  window, lowering them down by continuing to push
  my body backward from my bed out the window.
  Once my lower body is all the way out, I'll let
  my legs drop down by hanging on to my upstairs
  bedroom window ledge in kind of a pull-up
  position. This will mean my legs, from the shins
  down to my feet, will be hanging directly in front
  of the kitchen window downstairs if I stretch all
  the way out in the pull-up position.
- Dave will look up at some point from doing the
  dishes in the kitchen sink, and see my ankles and
  feet hanging there. This will startle Dave. I'll
  even make my legs kind of stiff and dead, and
  swing them back and forth very slightly with my
  upper body. This is going to be great. Dave is
  going to freak out when he looks up.

I start the plan. Everything is going great. I quietly
prop the window open. I can still hear Dave doing the

dishes. He hasn't heard a thing. I start pushing my body
out. The windowsill scrapes slowly past my ankles, then
shins, then legs, then thighs. My boxer shorts get stuck for
a second, but then the windowsill is scraping slowly past
my waist, then oh my God . . . faster now. Faster past my
stomach, then my chest, and ripping faster still. I'm still
groggy, but a sudden rush of adrenaline makes me realize
I am falling. I get an idea: Quick! Get ready to grab the
window's ledge so you'll stop the skidding and drop into
the pull-up position. Oh, no. I can't make a grip with my
hands, I haven't been awake long enough. The muscles
won't make my hands grip. In a split second, the wood
and splinters race up and rip past my armpits, then arms
and forearms, and I am starting a fast fall from the second
story. I try to somehow grab on to the side of the house
like a cat or something, but it's no use. The upstairs wood
and paint start racing by fast, then the strip of wood trim
that separates the first and second story of the cottage
scrapes over me like a violent speed bump. I wake
up enough to think, "I am falling down the side of the
house." The kitchen window suddenly races by and I catch
a glimpse of Dave's wide-eyed expression. The look on his
face scares me. Fear hits me. In a split slow-motion second
that seems to take four minutes, I realize that I will be
landing in nothing but my underwear on the side of the
house that is thick with thorn bushes, and berry vines,
and lumber and refuse ditched there years ago and probably left over from when the people in the main house
built this place. There is not even enough clearance to
walk where I will be falling. You wouldn't be able to walk
a path down that side of the cottage even if you were

wearing boots, jeans, and long sleeves. You would need to cut your way through there with a steel rake or chainsaw, the thorn bushes and vines are so thick. In about five-eighths of a second I will be landing there in my most worn-out pair of boxers, the ones that have been retired to the "for sleeping alone in only" category. I brace for hitting the ground. Vines and dirt and sky are spinning around and then I hit hard. Silence. Pain. I hear somebody from the park that borders the cottage say, "What the hell was that? Did you see that?" Then I hear Dave laughing somewhere inside the cottage as he runs to the door and opens it, and lets it slam behind him. He sounds scared but is still laughing, and at the same time yelling my name. I lie there hoping that I have startled him.

I had been spending most of the days leading up to my interview thinking about what I would accept for a salary. I kept in mind that I would have a lot of time off when the show was not taping. That's all part of the deal. I racked my brain with the numbers. I added up how much it would cost to buy the things I needed:

- Couch for the cottage, some new CDs, a better mountain bike, more bottle rockets.
- Small refrigerator for my bedroom so I wouldn't always have to climb down the ladder to go to the kitchen for a Coke or a beer (or even ice cream if I wanted to fork over an extra twenty-five for one with a little freezer).
- Basic stuff for my office at the TV studio, including a small stereo and duplicate copies of

my favorite CDs from home, so I wouldn't be in the middle of writing a sketch at the office and looking for the perfect CD to listen to and then have to realize, "Oh, I think that's at home."

The way I figured it, I would have enough to pay for it all with even the lowest offer they could make me. As for now, I barely had enough to buy a button-up Gap shirt for my interview.

When I walked into the lobby at the local network affiliate's offices, I realized I was accidentally about thirty-one minutes early. There were pictures of the big network daytime soap opera stars framed and some even signed. And a picture of Rikki Lake, and next to her a picture of a network affiliate star named Erica "Ricky" Rivers, who was just as good (totally just as good) and who hosted a hit daytime talk show in this market. And there were pictures of the *Big Crazy Night Live* cast. The people I would be writing for. Almost my colleagues. Almost *my* cast, if you will. Practically already the people without whom none of this would have ever happened for me. The front desk receptionist jarred me back to reality and told me that the producer would see me now.

I walked past the television broadcasting studio full of local women complaining to Erica "Ricky" Rivers that a diet high in sugar had made them commit violent acts against noisy neighbors. Ms. Rivers told them in a very firm tone and in no uncertain terms that they were going to have to give up the sugar in order to kick the habit of being a neighborhood menace. I walked down the long hallway and was shown to a small office and told that the producer would be there in a moment. I waited and enjoyed the pictures of his friends and family that were on his walls while listening to the easy-listening jazz on the small, cube-shaped radio that played on his desk and displayed pictures of his children.

(Thinking: He has been expecting you for a few days now. He is looking forward to this as much as you are. Take his first offer. Don't look like you're jumping at the offer. Appear to be *considering* the offer. But take the offer. This is not about money. You will only be here a short while anyway, and then there will be *Saturday Night Live* and more money than you know what to do with.)

(Playing on desktop photo cube radio: instrumental version of "The Way It Is," by Bruce Hornsby and the Range. A sign, even though there are no lyrics present. Even though the song might have nothing to do with what I'm feeling. Okay, not a sign. Calm, calm, calm. You are a young tree in the breeze without a care. You are calm, you bend . . . calm . . .)

"Hi, I'm glad you came by. Nice to meet you."

(Now thinking: What? Hell yes, I came by! I'm wearing a button-up Gap shirt, for chrissakes! It isn't so much that I came by . . . it's more that I have *arrived!*)

Was this guy not getting it? Or maybe I was dressed too well for this? Oh, no. That's it, isn't it? I'm not dressed right for a writer. These television comedy writers, they're supposed to be a daring and dangerous bunch. Mostly men who inject mixtures of heroin and whiskey into their eye so they don't have to stop freebasing cocaine to have a drink and some smack, and then they write a brilliant dark-comedy sketch about an armless clown on fire or something, right? I am too tame by comparison, right? Is that the problem? Is that what's going wrong already? I mean, when this guy was on the phone leaving me a message four days ago, he was probably holding the phone between his chin and shoulder, looking for something to cook some heroin up in, and trying to figure out where he left his office hooker, right?

He sat down in his ergonomic chair, reached across the desk, and adjusted the tuning on the square radio where his friends and family were smiling back at us, so that the light contemporary jazz came in without the intermittent ribbon of static that starts to occur on a cloudy day. Static . . . music . . . music with less static . . . music with even less static now . . . one last little blast of static and then . . . FM: no static at all.

Perfect. Okay. Relax.

I can just be myself.

Well, maybe not myself, because television comedy people were, as I was saying, something faster and darker and maybe more fearless than myself. I had read the dust jacket of that book by Woodward about Belushi. I'm sure I've retained enough to fake my way through this job interview. And there's *Permanent Midnight* guy, Jerry Stahl, the writer who spent his time copping dope and wishing he could beat the hell out of the Alf puppet. He was fierce and he was comedy and darkness and a real television writer, and I can be like him. I can do this. I steadied myself like a young actor playing an American badass for the first time after portraying a mild-mannered young man for the last twenty-five seasons. I would open my mouth and the darkness would just come out. And so I opened it.

"Well, thank you. Nice to be here. Thank you for your call."

We started talking as he adjusted the screen saver on his computer. I think there was something with underwater fish swimming by, and he wanted to make the underwater bubble noises stop coming from it.

"Do you know how to get this thing to stop making those noises?"

"Um, I think you have to open the control panel on the Apple menu, and then choose Sound, and then choose Mute."

As it turned out, he didn't realize that it would mute all of the computer's sounds.

"Well, then I can't hear that little sound that tells me I have e-mail."

He kind of had a point, so he ended up settling on a plain green background without sounds. He asked me if I knew how people put pictures of their family or of ski trips on there, but I didn't. He continued to look for ways to do this, and then . . . we got down to business. He told me he liked the scripts, which was good. He told me they get a lot of stuff sent in, and most of it never really catches his eye, but that my stuff did . . . which was good. And then he made me an offer.

"You want something to drink? Coke? Diet Coke? Water? Coffee?"

I don't remember what I chose; I only remember that as I opened it, the producer said that he would hire me . . . *if we were in New York or Los Angeles.* He explained that the network affiliate simply doesn't have the money to hire new writers.

"But what about, like, being a page? One of those people in the blue blazers who gives tours of the studio and stuff?"

He told me that was really only a major-network thing . . . in New York or Los Angeles. Still, I could've sworn there was a guy giving a studio tour when I walked in there. But the producer assured me that, basically, they could only afford to pay him and the five or six other people who worked on the show. There was almost no hope of getting hired. He told me that there was only one way that would change.

"Basically, the only way there's going to be a job opening on the show is if somebody dies," he said, laughing.

I sat there sipping my soda. I could feel my eyebrow arch, and while the producer tried to figure out how to add photographs of his family to his computer desktop, I was staring at the side of his head and thinking. I could stab the side of it. I could set the hair on it on fire. I could somehow snap it quickly, or put a bag over it really fast and smother him before he knew what happened.

And then I came to my senses. I wasn't going to kill anybody to get a job. I just sat there, once again feeling like I wasn't driven enough to get what I wanted and just thinking, Well, I guess I must not want it badly enough.

The host of the show poked his head in to say hello. And, of course, I recognized him, although at the moment he was not dressed as a woman, and he was not dressed as a kung fu fighter, and he was not a news anchorman doing the update. We would end up spending time together. He's a funny guy, this guy. We would spend most of our time together drinking whiskey and beer and talking about how nobody would get a job on that show until somebody died, and then he would have one last drink and make the long drive home. I would take a cab. And sometimes we would go to lunch and talk about comedy and comedy writing, and how the business works. And so one afternoon we're at a place that has a phrase for a name. I can't recall the exact name/phrase.

- My God It's Friday Again and Part of Me Is Dying?
- When Friday Comes We Will Eat Nachos While Something Inside of Us Grows Toward Disaster?
- It's the End of the Week and I'm Still Getting Gypped?

I don't know. The name's probably not important right now. A little girl comes up to the table we're sitting at, and recognizes who is sitting across the table from me.

"Can I have your autograph?" She holds out her place mat, on which she has drawn a picture of him.

I sit there feeling like something not quite famous enough to be noticed by kids. I am the Muppet that didn't make it past the first audition. I am the Teletubby that was kicked out of the group right when they got signed to a TV deal. I'm a less popular off-brand facsimile in her eyes. I am Gum-Eye, "a Gumby-type action figure" wrecked by the guilt that comes with half hoping somebody you like and think is funny would create a job opportunity by dying. I am all of this and invisible until she says this:

"Are you famous, too?"

"Well, I'm not too famous. I sure like your drawing, though. Are you a famous artist?"

She runs away laughing, gets another paper place mat, and runs back to us. She holds it out and says, "Can I have your autograph, too?"

And I sign my name on a blank white paper place mat.

"I can draw you on there," she says.

"No."

She starts drawing and I am afraid to see what she will arrive at. Everything is so obvious to children. They can see through anything you try to fake and right through to the real you. This scares the hell out of me. I mean, what is she filling the place mat with, pictures of me alone smoking stale Camel Lights, eating a Cup O' Noodles, and checking the mail repeatedly? To my relief, she draws me as a kind-looking stick figure, with a slightly misshapen head, kind of a large nose, and a weak chin. She has made her point and it does not go unnoticed by me. The stick figure is smiling, though, and I sign my name on it.

I sat in the producer's office a little bit longer. I was staring at the side of this man's head while he played with his computer and told me that my comedy writing was good, and then it was time for one of those awkward walks to the door where I tell him it was nice to meet him, and we kind of stand there. I don't know what he's thinking, but I'm thinking about what I would say if I were the guy giving the studio tour:

[Let group gather in corner of studio where Ricky Rivers's show is taped. Remember to ask "icebreaker" question with a smile, otherwise it could be a little intimidating for the group.]

Erica "Ricky" Rivers Set

How many people have done some arguing and name-calling, and the loved one you were doing that to got mad and drove off in a car and was maybe killed in an accident and now you have that on your shoulders? Well, you may want to talk to Erica "Ricky" Rivers weekdays at three-thirty either as a caller or an in-studio guest right here on this studio set. Ricky is the Pacific Northwest's answer to the major-network female television talk-show hosts. She has helped area residents cope with everything from overeating to family members who dress like sluts, and she's been right here on Channel 11 KSEA for seven non-consecutive seasons.

[Walk everyone by the set and let them take a look at Ricky's desk and chairs.]

[Next stop is the editing booth. Let group stand in front of glass looking in at editors working.]

Editing Booth

Does anyone remember when a rather hungover Ron Johnson, host of the live morning program *Good Day, Seattle,* looked right at the camera, rubbed the sleep from his eyes, clipped on his small microphone, and, not knowing that his live cue had already been signaled, unwittingly started the show by declaring, "You should see some of the pigs I'll screw when I'm too hammered to know better. I don't care if they're men or women if I've got a quart of gin in me."

[Without fail somebody will raise their hand and answer yes to this one, even though the only way any account of the incident was broadcast was by way of local hearsay.]

Well, if you saw it in front of your eyes, it's only because the person telling you the story was giving you a really good, vivid description of this favorite local legend. Main editor Bob Kalin inside the booth here [tap on glass and Bob will wave] was the man responsible for catching the mishap in the nick of time and editing it out with our six-second delay. The only thing local viewers saw after six seconds of the show's logo graphic and theme music was an inexplicably embarrassed, stammering, shocked host explaining to viewers, "I'm a heterosexual man who favors monogamy but can still see true beauty in both men and women of all sizes, shapes, and colors. I am now aware that I needn't sexually make myself act out and ruin the beauty I see."

[Leave studio and head down the hallway of photos, back to lobby to end tour. As we pass by photos, maintain casual stroll and make following comments about people in photos.]

Some of the folks we're walking by you will recognize, and others you may not have seen before, because they're the people behind the scenes of the shows. Phil Pearce, for instance, the executive producer of *Big Crazy Night Live* or whatever it's called.

[Keep smile and pleasant stride. Hide contempt. This group is here for a fun tour, not a bitter recollection of your experience of not getting hired on a sketch comedy show.]

Yep, Phil Pearce, folks . . . paid, of course. On the payroll. Medical . . . dental . . . retirement plan and whatnot. Not hiring writers, I can tell you that much in case we have any aspiring television comedy writers in the group today. Different story maybe in New York or Los Angeles, but not much is going to happen for you here if you're thinking of television, folks. Okay. Fine. You move on, you know?

You just . . . move . . . on . . . folks.

[Take a second to let message sink in and then politely wrap it up, directing group to the gift shop and adjusting blazer, then clasping hands together gently behind you in an "at ease" posture.]

I go home and I get out of my job interview clothes and into the clothes I wear to the catering company job I recently started. The interview with the producer has made it important for me to reaffirm my position of never selling out. My friends don't need to hear that I'm not getting hired . . . I'll spin it to something more like: I am sticking to my guns and not selling out. Even though, you know, there isn't anybody buying. Later that night at work, I'm in the middle of a really, really turbulent speech about how everybody in Seattle has sold out and how I'm not, uh, going to. And as great as the speech is going, it's mostly lost on the older Hispanic man I am standing next

to as I wash the silverware while he dries. But something inside of me is telling me he kind of gets it, that
this is a universal language, because every now and then
he smiles and wipes his forehead and says something in
broken English like:

"The more . . . we wash the . . . more they bring
dirty to us."

"Absolutely, brother." I feel like at least one person is
listening. Sort of.

So, anyway . . . I'm right in the middle of fire and
brimstone and silverware and dishes and the moment is so
pure and a busboy lets me know I have a phone call. It's a
friend of mine. Before he can even ask how the interview
went, I let him know.

"Listen, basically a paycheck from some TV company does not mean a person is a success at a given—"

"So I was playing a tape of your little radio show
you were doing at KCMU and guess who thinks . . ."

He's been dating a woman I haven't met. But she's
great from what I hear. I don't know a lot, but I know
she's from Seattle and that she has recently taken a job at
MTV as a development executive, and so she's moving to
New York.

". . . you should audition at MTV? And before you
start your whole 'MTV is the man' thing, you should at
least consider going out there to—"

"Oh my God. This producer guy today was telling
me that if I just got to New York or L.A., I could get
something going. So she's thinking MTV, huh? Perfect.
Perfect. And I can do other stuff besides the whole VJ

thing, you know? I mean, like . . . I can work in some stuff about movies, and comedy. I could interview celebrities. Celebrities of all kinds, really, if you think about it."

FANTASY INTERVIEW WITH REESE WITHERSPOON

DAN KENNEDY: Your name sounds weird. It sounds weird when I say it out loud and it sounds weird when I say it in my head.

REESE WITHERSPOON: *[Nervous laugh]* Yeah, it's a little bit weird. People always ask if I changed my name. I'm always like, "Do you think I made this name up?!" My parents were always great. They always told my brother and me to be proud that our name sounded different.

DK: Reese Witherspoon. Reese Witherspoon. Reese Witherspoon. It sounds weirder the more you say it.

RW: *[More nervous laughter. Probably nervous about interview.]*

DK: Royce Tetherhoogin. Reecy Dwindlecork. Ryban Tattlehoosier, Screech Woodenspoon, Squeaky Wheelspinner, Peel Weatherstation . . .

RW: I guess . . . I'm wondering if you have any questions for me.

It was now imperative that I change my platform quickly. I would become the "only person in alternative rock and pop culture TV keeping it real." This was *not* selling out. This was *changing things from within*, and somebody had to do it . . . and it was gonna be me. And so I saved my money up ($418) and borrowed some from friends ($2,300) and I started thinking of what I should pack. And eventually I packed it up. And somewhere along the line, I started knowing that I wasn't coming back.

After I went up the escalator of 1515 Broadway, on my first day in New York, I found myself in my first conference room looking out over Times Square for the first time in my life, and a voice that I had *never* heard before came out of me. It was the voice of some guy who wanted this to work out. And when that guy clashed with the guy who was determined to never sell out, the results were strange. In my MTV auditions, I basically looked like a nice guy who wanted things to work out, who would suddenly get some kind of stomach cramps and be kind of pissed off. I would start to say something like, "All right, coming up we have the new video from the Smashing Pumpkins," and then in that three or four seconds when the camera was still on me, I would try to look tough and cool and intense all of a sudden. That's the part that looked like a stomachache.

I thought it was going like this:

ME: *[Mic is almost down throat]* Arrrrrre you reeeady, you tired, flabby, dreamless, and gutless masses?! This is the eye of the hurricane, and your kids are calling the shots starting now! This is anarchy!

When I looked at the audition tapes at the end of each day, it was clear that it was actually going more like this:

> **ME:** *[Looking very agreeable and eager]* Okay, my
> name is Dan Kennedy. Glad to be hang-
> ing out with you this afternoon. Coming
> up, we've got the new one from the Back-
> street Boys and also something from Busta
> Rhymes and Snoopy Dog Doggy, so stick
> around.
>
> **THEM:** CUT! Correction on the name. It's Snoop
> Doggy Dog.

I was thinking the mistake way actually sounded
pretty good. You get the extra *y* sound that way. Where
do these guys get the names? There's such a fine line
between a rap name that works and one that doesn't:

Rap Names That Don't Work
    Nutty Lad
    Ralph Mouth
    PBS
    Mr. Bubble
    Bea "Dolly" Maguire
    Mean Cab Driver
    Sweetie Pie

There was also the issue of my ad-lib body movements. Little moves I tended toward when they told me to
do something while the camera lingered before cutting
away to the commercial. Strange body movements somewhere between trying to appear happy to have things
work out (absentminded dancing/rotating) and trying to
keep a serious and intense expression on my face. These

are the moves that looked like the very early stages of food poisoning.

At one point, watching these tapes alone, I thought, What if being a VJ is the worst thing I could do? It turned out I had nothing to worry about. My "nice guy with intermittent stomach/neck pains" persona wasn't turning out to be much of a fit for the network, and basically another guy got the job. Turns out, his whole "nice guy who *doesn't* get jolts of intermittent stomach pain" persona was what the MTV people were after. But I was here now. I lived in New York. And I couldn't help but think about what that TV producer in Seattle told me about how it would be easier for me to get hired here.

9

New, Improved, and Easier to Use:

My Short Ride on Madison Avenue

While I was working at New York advertising agencies, occasionally someone would get my phone number, call me up, and ask me how to go about breaking into advertising as a copywriter. Before I could say much, they would eagerly inform me that they had gone to college, graduated with a degree in media or communications, and then attended a handful of reputable workshops that teach the business of advertising. That's when I would realize they had way more experience than me and that all they really had to do was send their résumé around town and take a few interviews, and then decide which job offer to accept.

Noting their credentials for the job they wanted, and my lack of credentials for the job I had, I also let them know that they shouldn't send their résumé to the agency I was working at.

"Yeah, well, I'm the guy who kind of does the hiring . . . and . . . you know . . . we just don't really need any copywriters at the moment. Probably not for the next few years," I would say.

"Wow."

"Yeah, there's just been a real . . . lack of new . . . things to sell to people, and so of course that means there are fewer advertisements being written this year, so, um . . . you know . . ."

And they were actually usually eager enough to please that they would really identify with this shortage of new or improved products in America.

"Yeah, I know. Man . . . I can remember when, you know, there was *always* some new thing that was being advertised. Some kind of new soap or some kind of improved soda . . . like clear Pepsi. Do you remember clear Pepsi?"

"Yeah, that stuff was pretty good. Listen, I should—"

"You liked it? In school we studied it as a bad example of extending a brand at the cost of an already relatively firm position in a competitive market."

"I was being sarcastic. I couldn't even believe Pepsi would think of, um, extending their . . . firm . . . market thing . . . or . . . whatever. Hey, I'm heading into a big presentation, so I should go. I hope my advice has been of some help."

When I was in their position, I had come to New

York to, well, uh . . . to audition to be a VJ. But the friend whose couch I was sleeping (living) on after arriving in New York said that she could bring me on where she worked. At an advertising agency. Perfect. This is where I could start. It's all shaping up, isn't it? Glamorous advertising agency hires guy. Guy becomes advertising icon, then moves into world of professional television comedy writing, looks back on start and says things like, "I recommend that people start in advertising. If you can work in a sixty-second format, you can work in any time frame, and that's what . . ."

So the plan was that I would go to work with her in the morning. And so I prepared by staying out the night before and drinking the rest of my Visa card at a bar in SoHo called the Cub Room. I told myself I could afford to do that since I was on my way to becoming a New York advertising icon starting the next day. And when the next day came at eight A.M., my future in New York advertising agencies was off to an unglamorous start in a Connecticut marketing agency. I sat down in front of the desk of the creative director. I was hungover, confused, wearing a leather jacket and black T-shirt on my top half, and conservative khaki slacks and sensible shoes on my bottom half. My top and bottom halves in battle to see which guy would win. Creative edgy guy, or sensible suburban guy? I hedged my bets by putting half of my money on creative edgy guy, and the other half on sensible guy. Who cares? Nobody was even taking book on it. Dramatic self-aggrandizing gambling analogy taken even further: *And everybody knows that when you hedge your bets, you always lose.*

"Heyyyyyyyy, it's the cool guy from Seattle," he said, seeing only the top portion of me.

"Oh, yeah?" I said, trying to act like I knew who he was talking about. Nirvana? On his headphones?

"Well, that's what I've been told," he said, taking off his headphones and shaking my hand.

"Oh, me?"

"What?" he said, still shaking it, me wanting to kindly explain that last night I drank the last third of my Visa card, and if I were shaken any more, I would vomit on him.

"'Oh, my' is what I meant. I meant, 'Oh, my . . . you're right. I'm that guy.'"

"Yep, you're the funny guy, all right! No argument here!"

I tried to recover. I might have. Just in time for him to hand me more pictures of beer than I ever thought I would have the stomach to see in the condition I was in.

"Can you make this stuff cool and funny, Mr. Cool Funny Guy?" He smiled.

I stared at the pictures of the beer. I was wondering if vomiting egg sandwich and Gatorade (from a deli on Seventh Avenue about three hours ago as I was ending my night) onto the pictures would make them any funnier.

"Yeah. I mean . . . these aren't very funny. So I, um, could make them funnier."

"Good. How much is your rate?"

(Running through my head: "One fifty. Say it. You *are* worth it. The worst he can say is no.")

"Tell you what. I'll pay you five hundred a day. That's what I pay my junior freelance copywriters."

(Now running through my head: "Don't look surprised now. Don't get really happy and cry, either. He
thought you were being silent because you know the rate
and you know the drill. Take the money. You'll be able to
work for two days and be set for a *month*.")

Wrong.

There is only one note of financial advice I am qualified to give anybody who happens to be reading this
book: You cannot work for two days and be set for a
month in New York. Not if your rate is five hundred dollars a day. In my very recent past as a slacker in Seattle,
yes, I could've. I could've worked for two months and
retired and sat on the small deck (shared with all tenants)
of my Seattle apartment building and thought about
whether or not I wanted to send my nonexistent children
to a private school. I could've worked for nine to eleven
business days and sent my nonexistent wife on vacations
and shopping sprees that I would hear about via cell phone
while I was on the golf course with imaginary friends who
were software moguls. In New York I did none of that on
five hundred dollars a day, especially when I initially refused to work more than three or four days a month (who
needs to when I'm making this outrageous fee?), and especially when I burned bridges by turning down job offers.

And so I sat there for the day and even for a second
day, looking at a picture of beer and thinking of funny
and cool headlines to write that would appear above the
beer in the picture, making the beer appear to be something that resembled the qualities described to me in
hours of meetings. They wanted this beer to be real beer
for real men. They wanted this beer to be the beer that

geeks don't drink. They wanted the headlines to make fun of geeks who drink beer that isn't cool. No problem, I thought, I'll just write down every insult that every cool person has ever slurred at me about the cheap, uncool beer I had spent my entire adolescence drinking.

- When you start drinking real beer, maybe we'll hang out sometime.
- You've had your first beer. Congratulations. Let us know when you have your first *real* beer.
- Ever wonder if women ignore you because they're embarrassed to be seen next to the beer you drink?
- Hey, Kennedy. You act like a complete reject. I swear to God, if you act like you know me when the girls get here, you'll be sorry. What are you supposed to be? Some kind of cool punk rocker? You're not really punk. And you're not really that cool, ass-bite.

The last one didn't make the cut. But as I found out the following day, I was a hit. I had arrived on the New York advertising scene. Well, I had arrived in Connecticut, anyway.

"We love what you did with the microbrew campaign." This from the director of all creativity after two days of my five-hundred-dollar-a-day genius writing.

I adjusted my new sunglasses ($175) and kicked off my blue Puma sneakers (only $12 a pair but one size too small—the man at the small stand on the edge of Chinatown said he could sell them so cheap because a bunch of size nines had fallen off of a truck, whatever that has to do with anything. At the low price I bought seven pairs for $85 no tax. He said he was able to make the deal since I wanted a pair in a different color for each day of the week).

"In fact," the creative director continued, "we want to get you to look at some of our other clients' stuff before you go home today. If you can make candy and soup as funny as beer, we need to talk."

I felt something change inside of me, a new confidence that I stammered under the power of. This is what I was meant to be. America needs its next Andy Warhol, and he wasn't going to be painting Campbell's soup cans on canvases in a downtown loft this time around. This time he would work his pop art magic by actually working on *the Campell's soup account.* I tripped over my excited tongue as it looked for the perfect phrase to showcase my newfound self-esteem.

"Well, good! That's what I like to hear! That's why I like it!"

He gave me a long look, sizing up the change in me. I tried to tone it down and remember where I came from. I felt myself get smaller again . . . if only to preserve the big success I had found.

"Well, listen . . . are you looking for a full-time job? You want to come on staff?"

Oh, man. Oh, no. Oh, God. I wanted to laugh at the thought of it. How was I going to tell this guy that I was only going to be working three or four days a month on this kind of dough? I don't think he got it. He probably thought I needed more than a thousand a month to live on.

I sat there thinking about this guy in front of me wanting me to tell him that I was really in need of a full-time job. I thought about it. Come to think of it, I hadn't really gotten off my friend's couch and found an apartment yet, and from what I had heard, they were pretty expensive in New York. And at some point I was probably going to have to pay taxes on this crazy dough I was making. Uncle Sam would want a cut of these heady two-thousand-dollar months.

"I'm really not a nine-to-five kind of guy, man. I work a few days a month, and you know . . . that's about it. I need time for other stuff."

He tried to make the deal attractive. He asked if I could stay a few more weeks.

"Weeks!" I laughed.

He laughed, too, for some reason. Oh, what the hell. I needed to get a little extra pay built up to get an apartment. And so I came around for a few more weeks. I laid off the shopping, even though my look was important to me now that I was working in the advertising (okay, direct mail) business, which is essentially all about being in New York (Connecticut in this case, but I was just starting) and capitalizing on image. I had to make it clear that I had the image. The Puma sneakers. The colorful top brand of motorcycle-racing jacket. I was new. I was improved. It cost a little more, but I was worth it. I was finally ready to Just Do It.

"Sure, I can come around for a few more weeks while you look for somebody who needs a steady job."

And in the remaining weeks I continued coming into work with my friend, but I no longer needed to sleep on her couch. I had found an apartment. And so after spending my days in Connecticut making America's favorite durable goods somehow funnier and cooler by writing headlines for pieces of mail and Sunday newspaper circulars that would feature ads for the products, I would come home to an apartment in Manhattan. My work was coming in handy on several accounts at the agency. I had gone from beer to soup, then candy bars, and finally credit-card direct-mail advertisements—I wrote the headline on the outside of the envelope *and* the letter inside that invited folks to apply for the credit card. And then my stint was over for a few weeks. Time to relax and take in the city while thinking about other pursuits without being stifled by the man. The system might work for others, but I was better off working only when I wanted to.

Man! Holy God! I had found a small apartment, and it turns out my damn rent and utilities came to well over two thousand dollars the first month. Okay. Think. Jesus. I need to get a job. After being home for about a week, I started to panic. I would add and re-add my finances. Sometimes there were glorious mistakes in my favor. I won't soon forget the short-lived rush of adding up my bills and then adding up my five-hundred-dollar days, only to find that even after I paid everything for the month, I would have fifty thousand dollars left. I sat there open to the seduction of my success until I realized I had done something completely wrong with the decimal or the division key or something, but still—that was a sweet, sweet moment killed only by equally accidental accuracy after re-adding and re-subtracting. Accuracy was less kind and made me realize I had better call the agency in Connecticut and schedule my next work, so that I could sleep nights. There was only one problem: My phone wasn't hooked up yet. Okay, it was hooked up, but there was some kind of block on long distance. I tried sending a fax on the new fax machine I had bought, but I guess the long-distance block worked on the fax, too. So I used a neighbor's phone. ("Yours is still working, huh? Yeah, because I talked to 2B and they said theirs was out. Mine's out. Huh? Oh, this? I bought this when I first got to New York. It's supposed to be the best racing jacket made. That's what the guy said.")

But there was another problem. The agency had hired somebody. For a minute, I regretted not having taken that job.

Still, I refused to wallow in regret, so instead, I put all of my energy into panicking and imagining how I was going to die without money and most likely in the streets after losing my apartment. The bottom of the depression came when I was sitting at my makeshift dinner table filling out a credit-card application that had arrived in the mail, hoping to get some credit to tide me over until I booked more work. I skipped the introductory letter and went straight to the application. I didn't need to waste my time reading the stupid letter since I was the guy who had written it. My God, I had no idea that I was writing a letter to a frightened version of myself sitting in a tiny apartment in Manhattan when I cranked this seductive upbeat prose out a month ago in Connecticut.

Then I went downstairs, dropped the application in the mail, and bought a copy of *Adweek* magazine so I could search the help-wanted ads. There was a small agency in Manhattan looking for a copywriter. The ad said that if you didn't have attitude, you wouldn't be the writer for the job; that the right writer would be able to use very few words to convey the most powerful concepts and ideas. I wrote a cover letter to the small agency and faxed it that afternoon.

> *To Whom It May Concern:*
> *Hire me or I will kick your ass.*

In the meantime, while I was waiting to hear back, I called a friend of a friend who worked in the business and told her I needed some help getting some job interviews. She was a really successful television commercial producer and could get me into the biggest agencies in town.

"Do you have a portfolio that you can take in to interviews?"

"Oh . . . uh, yes. Yes, I have my, you know, port-folio . . . which should work . . . for that."

(Inside my head: "Make some sort of portfolio. Kinkos?")

"Great. I'll call some people."

The only piece of produced work I had a copy of was a direct-mail piece for a credit card, and I had dropped that into a mailbox about an hour ago. So, being that I had never seen a portfolio, I figured if I printed out the pages filled with the headlines that the people in Connecticut thought were so good, you know, that would probably be what a professional portfolio looked like. I spent a little extra and made a little color logo out of my initials for the "cover" of this stack of five pieces of paper with typewritten headlines on them. Sort of spent a little extra to show I was a pro. Been around the block. Image. Play it. It would be a long time before I got a look at what a professional advertising portfolio looked like. Once I did get a look at a proper advertising portfolio, I would note the differences . . . but it would be too late by then. I would see that it's supposed to be big. It's supposed to have colorful advertisements from popular magazines in it. It's leather, not paper. You're generally supposed to have three or four of these portfolios so that they can be in several places at once. I would not know that until way after the damage was done. My friend called me back later that week.

"Can you be at Madison and Fifty-second for an interview in thirty minutes? You're meeting with the partners of one of the biggest agencies in New York, and I've told them you're great and they want to meet you. Bring portfolios, because I have four more places for you to hit after you leave. Just call me when you're leaving there and I'll tell you where to head to next."

When I walked into the agency, I was rushed right into the guy's office whose name appears not only on his office door, but also on the front door of the agency, and on the elevator plaque, and on the cover of respected trade magazines. The big guy. I couldn't believe the treatment I was being given. Calls were being sent to voice mail. Meetings were being ordered to start without him. I sat a little suspicious trying to imagine what a friend of my friend had told this guy about me. And then I remembered, after small talk plagued with my little confused winces of paranoia and suspicion, that I was a success and

I had to act the talk. Or walk the talk. Or whatever they say about acting better than you think you really are.

"Well, I understand you are the man to meet if I'm looking for a creative genius."

(In my head: Do it. You are it. You are *not* as bad at this as you think you are. Maybe you learned as much in three and a half days of doing this as some people learn in three and a half years of doing it. Maybe failing classes has always been due to the fact that you're a genius and learning is too *easy* for you.)

I was still quiet and thinking, and this was misunderstood as some kind of quiet self-confidence.

"Perfect. A modest genius. I'll be quick, because I have ten places to be fifteen minutes ago."

I laughed way too hard when he said this. Apparently, it wasn't as funny as I thought, judging by his being startled by my loud laughter. I was still laughing pretty strong when I realized he wasn't, really. I tried to cover.

"Ha. Wow, sorry about that; it's just that sometimes a really funny ad idea pops into my head when I least expect it. Just thought of a good one, there. Right when you mentioned your schedule, I just remembered this great thing I worked on that was so funny. Okay . . . ha . . . anyway, you were saying?"

"I was saying that I need one guy who has what it takes to be an ECD—that's an executive creative director—and basically be in control of a piece of business that's worth about thirty-two million to my agency. He needs to be a miracle. Needs to be a great creative as well as a great account executive with lots of client contact."

"Rock it up on," I blurted loudly and nervously, trying to muster some excitement and confidence.

(Pause. He was just staring. I was very still, hoping the tongue-tied words would somehow disappear from the air between us.)

"What?" he asked, and I realized my nervous stab at coming up with a confident and motivational phrase had failed.

I tried again. "Let's get it up!"

Oh, no. Cover. Fast. Now. "That's why I like big bucks, I mean . . . that's what I would expect to hear . . . you know, that's . . . what I . . . like."

"Yeah." Pause. "Well . . . let's have a look at your portfolio."

The last thing I remember was tossing my five sheets of stapled-together 8½-by-11-inch paper onto his desk. I remember the gray-and-maroon "DK" logo landing on his desk. I remember him pausing again. He picked it up. He looked at me. I remember him leading me to the door with a smile that seemed strange and strained and maybe even frightened. There was something so incomplete about the visit to me. And so I stood there. He stood there. He thanked me again. I thanked him again. We both stood there still. He looked at me. I looked at him and spoke my last line: "I need to take that with me for another interview. I can bring it back if you need me to."

The rest of the day was spent in very similar interviews. The reactions ranged from a quick handshake once they saw the little portfolio thing I made, to one man who actually just started cracking up. I thought it was like one of those scenes in a movie where I'm supposed to reluctantly join in the laughter with the big guy, and so I did, and he laughed more, just like in the movies, and I laughed more with him. But then I was at the door again. How did I always end up at the door with these guys, not sure of what to say? I just ended up there like one of *The Brady Bunch* when they came home from a date: standing at the door not sure of how to end the evening now that we're back from the drive-in movie.

I got a call from the small agency that I faxed my brief cover letter to. We scheduled an interview. Apparently my letter exhibited the exact qualities of the perfect candidate. I was hired, even though I forgot to bring my portfolio to the interview. Or maybe because I forgot it. I thought it was important to make a few big gestures right off the bat to establish myself. After getting set up and settled in, I took the agency's biggest client to a strip club. I talked two or three of the other employees into coming along. Once we had finished our first round of drinks, it was brought to my attention by our almost naked waitress that my card just about reached its limit (it had been pretty abused in my jobless lurch), and that I was only able to put the first round of drinks on it. I explained to the other two employees that if they would get cash advances for the dancers from the handy ATM near the bar, as well as make sure our table had drinks on it for the night, I would see to it that the agency reimbursed them for the charges via my expense account, since I was a creative director and had a presumably more liberal expense account than they did. After charging around a thousand dollars between our three cards, only forty-one or so of which fit on my card, I learned the next morning when I went into work that I didn't really have an expense account to speak of. I mean, I could order staplers and tape dispensers and things for my office, but not a thousand dollars' worth of nightlife for a client they had already taken to a nice dinner earlier that evening. For whatever reason, the partners of the agency (three women and a gay gentleman) decided to be generous, compassionate, and fair beyond belief after having a series of meetings behind closed doors. They told me that they would actually reimburse me for half of the charges. I don't think they understood that the charges were all on other employees' cards, but still . . . this was the best news I could've hoped to get in my first year of employment. I was ecstatic. It felt like winning some kind of advertising award. The only awkward thing left for me to do was to quietly make the rounds to the other employees' cubicles and explain to them that I was mistaken about the financial arrangements of last night's outing, and that they would only be getting half of that money back. I offered to pay the other half of the charge on their cards, but I knew that because of the debt I had run up while turning down job offers and working only three days a month, my paychecks would be pretty much spent for the next six months. I explained that I could take care of the charges in around seven months or so.

They looked at me still hungover and maybe somewhat frightened and confused, but seemingly somehow okay with the way things had turned out. I stood there wondering if this was what it felt like if you are one of those people who have leadership qualities. Bet you anything this is exactly how it feels.

A FEW OF THE LIES I'VE TOLD YOU AS AN ADVERTISING COPYWRITER

- A particular brand of quality sunglasses could completely change the way you perceive your life and yourself.
- People are noticing something unappealing about your body and they aren't telling you about it. And if you start eating a particular brand and type of yogurt, they will stop talking about the unappealing thing they are noticing, and start complimenting you.
- Recording your favorite songs onto a particular brand of blank CD is the best step to take if you're interested in controlling most or all aspects of your fate, and will almost always prevent unrequited crushes.
- Your children would rather have other parents based solely on the fact that you aren't serving meals that are as fun as the meals being served by your neighbors, but if you purchased these frozen meals, your family would be somehow better and more fun, like the neighbors whom your kids love more than you.
- If you have a sincere interest in Irish culture, you would attend a rock concert festival being sponsored by a popular Irish beer, and being held at a large outdoor concert facility in New Jersey.
- Using a particular credit card would enable you

not to have an office job, and instead have your own company, which would be run from your portable computer, from a patio next to a swimming pool.

NAMING A BREAKFAST CEREAL

This cereal was aimed at people in their thirties, who (research shows) associate breakfast with balance and spirituality. I was the copywriter who would be trying to give it a name. Never mind that I'm the least balanced individual in the building on any given day.

My best work ended up boiling down to this:

ALTAR

Agency said this one was "too demonic" and most commonly reminded people in focus groups of these five things:

1. Satan
2. Sacrifice
3. Death or dying
4. Catholicism
5. Marriage

TRANQUIL MORNING

Agency said it sounded too much like Nyquil and we'd get hassled by the Food and Drug Administration. Focus groups most commonly associated name with these five things:

1. Christmas

2. Laxatives
3. Nursing homes
4. Hangover cure
5. Pregnancy

RISE

Agency said they kind of liked it, but name seemed to imply a caffeinated burst of energy. Focus group said it made them think of:

1. Christianity and rising from the grave
2. Pharmaceutically induced erections
3. A rush or "speeding up"
4. Inflation
5. Rice

ENLIGHTEN

They loved it, but needed to check how much they would have to reduce the number of calories, according to FDA standards, to qualify the product as "reduced calorie" and then they could spell it "En *lite* en."

The next assignment was to work on finding a tag line for the cereal.

By five-thirty I was tired, and all I had was this:
Tag lines for En *lite* en:

- Wake up whenever you want.
- Nothing can hurt you now.
- Nothing is working out right and you don't care.

FOUR LINES THAT THE COPYWRITER OVERHEAD IN THE ELEVATOR

- "They're telling us that they can make its arms move, but they can't make it talk unless we get the heads made by this other manufacturer, and that manufacturer happens to be part of their company. So we told them to just worry about making the arms move right now, and we'll figure out what we want to do about making the head talk by the end of this week."
- "Steve didn't sign off on it, because Steve knows I like it, and Steve can't approve anything that he knows I like, because Steve is a bitch."
- "It's basically about depression. But they want to find a way to make it kind of funny, or at least fun to watch."
- "They wanted everybody to pitch in thirty bucks for a gift and lunch for her on Friday, and I'm only here for two weeks. I just said, 'Well, I can't make it, so just tell her the temp in Account Planning says Happy Birthday.'"

HOW I FAILED AT FLIRTING WITH A CUTE GIRL WHO WORKED AT THE AD AGENCY

- Telling her that I don't like going to parties because the only reason to go is to get drunk or laid.
- Trying to act like I knew a lot about the weather and restaurants in Boston when she spoke of

growing up there, even though I've only been to Boston once, and only to Logan Airport, and only for an hour.

- Saying, without prompting, that I could never be a drug dealer.
- Referring to some people I said hello to at a company party as friends, only to see them clearly try to figure out who I was and whether or not they knew me from work.
- Complimenting her in a snapshot of people at the beach that is taped to her computer that she apparently doesn't appear in.
- Complimenting her on the hilarious collection of kitsch canned-food items on her desk, only to find out they were donations to a holiday food drive for needy families.

UNPOPULAR NAME-BRAND CONSPIRACY THEORIES AND MYTHS

- Most cold and flu medications relieve symptoms more effectively and faster than they claim to. That's because most major pharmaceutical companies also own businesses that you can't enjoy while suffering a cold or flu: amusement parks, bike shops, stuff like that.
- There is a popular brand of lip balm that makes your lips feel a slight tingle. That's because the company that manufactures it also owns several people who are saying bad things about you.
- A popular brand of cola used to contain small

amounts of cocaine. That's because, at that time, the company also owned three popular nightclubs, and wanted to sleep with you and your best friend at the same time.

- There is a brand of fig cookie that contains trace amounts of rodent feces in its filling. That's because the company that makes it also owns a company that sells rodent feces cookies, which are packaged at the same facility.

ANONYMOUS COMMENT CARDS ABOUT A TV AD FROM EVERYDAY PEOPLE IN A PAID SURVEY

- I did not believe that a cat would be this smart, or be able to operate a pager or organizer or whatever that was. I would buy it if I liked the product.
- I know this is supposed to be funny . . . but does not take a genius to see that they aren't really talking and that the cat has fake legs and tail.
- Bird never talks about the cost of service or software after you buy it. Also, if you can do trick photography to make bird talking to cat, couldn't you make cat kill it somehow?
- SUCK IT GOOD, BABY! METALLICA RULEZ 4-EVAH!! I JUST MADE FIFTY $$ U LAME ASS!
- I would ask you to consider the bird's motivation for using product to get help instead of just flying away when cat chases it. That's honestly where it stops working for me. Also if this voice-over is just a scratch track, you should contact me

about doing voice of bird *or* cat. I have been
the baby in Babywipers spot as well as various
aliens and animated spokescharacters for top
packaged goods and entertainment accounts.

- Make cat funnier. Make him swear when bird
comes around? Dress him up in something? Cross-
eyed? It just seems like as long as you can totally
control cat, you should get him to do as many
weird things as possible when he's on-screen.

- I love your birds and the your cats and it will be
comedy. I would want this for being my job, can
this return here tomorrow in the day? Much
pleasure for loving something this amusing!

- I don't use computers or cell phones or e-mail.
Seems like another thing I don't need. Glad
birds like it.

10

www.myfirstmillion.com

Short attention spans are rewarded. Dyslexia is an impressive attribute, and completely unconventional thinking bordering on Down's syndrome is celebrated. You are encouraged to dress poorly and keep odd hours. Skip showering if you prefer, work at home, in bed, at the beach, anywhere you want because there is no "there" there, so you couldn't be "here" even if you wanted to be. Oh, and the ideas you have don't have to be ideas that are making money in order for you to get tons of money. Also, if you have dropped out of college, that's great—so did the guy who started Microsoft, and he is second only to the President of the United States in power. And he is wealthier.

Ho. Ly. Christ.

Sign me on, log me up, jack me in . . . whatever the hell you call it, just get me in the door. Because there will never be another time in history when the likes of me, the polar opposites of Malcolm Forbes, are winding up on the top of his list and on the cover of his magazine. This has got to be the only time in American history when you practically have to be a loser to win. If there is a time for me, then the Internet is clearly my time, period. Basically, if you are a cross between a mildly retarded petty thief, Rain Man, and a corner crack dealer who considers sleeping and hygiene a waste of valuable and potentially productive time—buy a laptop and let's get going.

Know that at this point in the Internet revolution, I am already learning regret. For instance, I regret having been the part-time restaurant worker in Seattle who was clearing the dirty glasses from the table of a friend from Canada who was then (1995) just starting what turned out to be an Internet company he would sell for millions.

"The Internet is a glorified CB radio. It won't be around in five years, trust me. And if you want any appetizers with your drinks, you should order now because the kitchen's closing."

And then on one of those days of sitting and regretting, the phone in my tiny office at the advertising agency rang. It was that very friend of mine from Seattle telling me he was moving to New York to start a new Internet company, and would I consider being part of the new company, even though I had expressed such a strong desire to not come onboard his last company when he was starting it? And of course there would be money. People were giving money away. There was money everywhere. They had even been inventing new terms like *centimillionaire* for people who had more money than could be described by good old-fashioned terms or phrases like *millionaire* or *millionaire several times over*. Terms and phrases that had, up to now, worked just fine. But the money wasn't what I was going into it for. It was for something else. Some, like, passion, or something. I guess. Whatever. Anyway . . .

I spent my last days in my tiny office at the advertising agency—a tiny office that smelled of cleaning products and mops—daydreaming of how my life was going to change. Images of getting into a hot tub filled with famous people at my Aspen chalet were downloaded and streamed through my fancy, new super-slim computerized mind along with pictures of me addressing the current crop of MIT graduates and letting them know that "these are remarkable times. Times when anything is possible. Times when you realize that maybe you weren't meant to be a rock star, or a songwriter like the ones in Texas, or an MTV personality, or a successful advertising agency employee, and instead of feeling like a failure, you can go on to change the way people are entertained in the world-wide . . . Internet . . . new media, convergence, e . . . thing . . . or whatever."

I knew about all of the venture capital out there. So I played it real cool when my friend asked if I would like to come be a part of the new company he was starting.

"Oh, I don't really know. I've done pretty well. Not sure I can make a move right now," I casually said into the phone that was pressed between my shoulder and ear, leaving my hands free to absentmindedly toy with a package of urinal cakes that had been left in my office by the last executive who had it.

"Yeah, I'm sure you're doing pretty well. We probably can't match the cash you're making . . . but is your job at the agency giving you any stock options?"

Oh my God.

They weren't.

I was being had! Robbed in the brick-and-mortar world like all the rest of them! I had to jump ship! The question in my mind wasn't, "How can I leave this job for way less than what I'm making?" No . . . that wasn't the question at all. The question I was asking myself was, "If this advertising gig is so sweet, why don't I have a centi-million shares of stock in the company?"

The idea for the new business was simple. It was comedy based. A humor venture. We would e-mail people the funniest things we found on the Internet. Things like jokes and funny video clips. We would find these things or people would send them to us, and then we would send them out to other people who wanted them [blah, blah, blah, bunch of fancy business-plan talk goes here] . . . and then . . . RICH. I figured that we would probably have to do most of the work ourselves for the first few months, but after that I would just have to call in from Aspen or Paris or something to make sure the guys we hired were e-mailing funny things out to people. Simple. There was a plan and a strategy and work to be done, but it was not to be my job to worry about any of that. I was not to be hassled with the business side of things. I would be the creative director, the guy who decides what stuff is funny and should be e-mailed out to our members, and how it should be mailed out, and maybe even what the Web site should look like.

I was the only American (it was just a Canadian, an Australian, and me) involved in the business, and so my insight into what was funny in American pop culture would be an integral part of making this thing tick. Plus, whatever work had to be done wouldn't be *hard* work, it would be *funny* work. Ahhhhhh, *funny* work . . . no problem. Just a matter of having a few laughs and sending out some e-mail—all stuff that I already knew how to do. I could laugh. I could send e-mail. My time had clearly come. And I know that's a tired notion at this point. Because it hasn't come. Not guitars, not fishing tournament trophies, not espresso vending cart ownership, not minor cable celebrity, not any of it. But there's something to admit here. Something that could change my luck entirely. Something to say once quickly and then move on. Or maybe once daily and then move on:

> *Drank like a fish since age sixteen, and later took*
> *a liking to anything from the dentist's and doctor's*
> *that made the alcohol work EVEN BETTER!*

Yeah, big secret, right? Like you couldn't tell something was up when I was huffing through a half case of whipped cream a day in that espresso chapter. Anyway, the big deal is that I have managed to quit. Or better put:

It has quit me. So the bottom line is the Internet revolution is here and I haven't had a drink or anything else for an entire year and I'm ready.

For the first few weeks, we just focused on all of the unfunny work, like making spread sheets that we could use to rate the jokes that we found on the Internet. I was a little concerned that we hadn't just gotten right into the funny part, and then into the rich part. But this stage probably wouldn't last long. We had conversations like this:

"Okay, I think we should send out the one about the lawyer who lisps and the prostitute who quit smoking going on vacation together," they would say.

"That's not funny, really," I would counter. "Why would a lawyer and a prostitute be spending Christmas together? It doesn't even make sense."

"Did you read the joke, Dan?"

"Yes."

"Well, maybe you should read it again because I don't think it had anything to do with Christmas."

"Well, it's to my understanding that the prostitute was spending the holidays with a lawyer, who as you mentioned has some sort of speech impediment, and who has also tried to stop smoking cigarettes. He says something to the prostitute about how he hasn't smoked during the holidays, and then she says—"

"Oh, okay. I see," said the Australian business school graduate who was already rich. "I thought they were *on holiday* together. In Australia if you're going on vacation, you say that you're going on holiday. So I thought this lawyer had found some scrubber to take with him on vacation."

"Scrubber?"

"Never mind. You're right, a lawyer and a hooker would never spend Christmas together. Let's rate that joke as a one. We'll only send it out if we don't have any twos or threes. See, the spread sheet sorts them automatically after you rate them. We can sort by keyword, too, so we can search for hookers, look for lawyers. We can file, say, drunk clergymen in another file. You really need to take some time to learn how to make these spread sheets in Excel. It'll make your job a lot easier. Maybe we could pay for you to take classes on using Excel for spread sheets."

For the next few months after that, we focused on more of the unfunny stuff, such as building lists of e-mail addresses of people to e-mail funny things to, once we got around to the part of finding funny stuff. We seemed a little behind schedule. I had originally thought we would have been just about getting done with the funny work at this point and already starting the rich part.

"Okay, Dan . . . how many names have you found for our list?"

"I thought people were going to join, so I haven't really . . . made people sign up . . . or anything."

"Well, people *are* going to join. But first we have to build a list of people to mail things out to, and then those people will forward the joke to other people, and so on, and so on. That's when people start joining because they want to get their own copy of the joke. So we need names to start."

Then for a few months we had meetings in our make-shift conference room about why people like funny things.

The meetings themselves weren't funny. My bosses wanted to figure out why people liked funny diversions on the Internet. Since we had been at this for five months at this point, I was hoping that maybe the deal was that if we could figure this part out, then the rich part would happen. I tried to make it as fast as possible by asserting the opinion that "people like funny things because funny things help them forget about painful realities like having money problems, and not liking their job that they thought would be more fun somehow, and how maybe none of their stock options seemed to be worth anything still, and how maybe they thought they would be in a hot tub filled with famous people or something, but all they seem to be doing is spending all of their time in meetings . . . and so, you know, if something is funny, at least it helps them, um . . . forget. Or whatever."

And we would "discuss" some of the things that people had actually started sending in to us. I was trying to remember that this was not a "them against me" situation, but it was hard.

> **THEM:** Okay, what did we think of the clip of Kermit the Frog in a porno film?
>
> **ME:** Was that other Muppet with him supposed to be Fozzy Bear?
>
> **THEM:** I don't know. We aren't that familiar with them. We aren't even sure we've seen them. I mean, aside from this.
>
> **ME:** I don't know if this clip is really that funny. You know, I mean . . . I grew up with those guys.

THEM: The guys that sent it to us?

ME: No. I mean, I grew up with the Muppets. And I liked them . . . so I guess this is kind of depressing. It's like seeing a friend from childhood who's fallen into a sad pattern of crack addiction and small-time crime or something.

THEM: Write that down! It's not funny if it's your friend from childhood, but maybe it would be funny if we made a clip maybe of this frog puppet smoking crack! Right?

ME: I didn't think it was funny when he was doing porno.

THEM: Who's doing porno?

ME: What? The frog, I mean.

A month or so went by of continuing to not find anything very funny. My attitude was getting worse by the day. There was some talk of me writing jokes myself, if I was so convinced that nothing we were finding or being sent was very funny. I gave it a shot, but everything I wrote had a punch line about giving up, or going broke, or death. I was clearly in no state to be writing cute jokes and riddles for the masses.

Another month went by, and I realized the only thing I seemed to be doing in my free time was talking to friends about how this wasn't working out. One day I was in bed typing e-mail to a friend of mine in Seattle whom I used to wash dishes with at a catering company, telling him about how this whole thing didn't seem to be working out. Halfway through typing the letter, I moved the laptop off of my lap, set it next to me on the bed, turned on the stereo, and drifted off to sleep. Almost like a little faux suicide. I think that was the beginning of the end for me as a dot-com centimillionaire. I watched it unfold in my mind as I fell to sleep, like a daydream about the tragic end to the Silicon Alley pop star legend's life that I never lived.

He was found in New York, lying on his bed, arms outstretched next to what may be a first for his generation: a suicide e-mail, on a laptop sitting next to him, composed of subject lines from the junk e-mail he had received:

Are you covered in the event of death
I used to be broke, but now I am
Superman With Viagra!
It's not too late!
Full Time
A Better Life

Outstanding Ski Vacations
All types of home loans
The Caribbean on $72 a day
Free ink cartridges and Motorola cell phones

But Time Is Limited
Finally the truth comes out
A revolutionary simple system
Everything must go!
You have been removed.

And so all we're left with is a note to an older Hispanic man in Seattle whom he used to wash dishes with

long before the wired dot-comedy e-mail business days of
heady fortune. He was young and he was wealthy. He was
a deflated man in his note. He spoke of seeing his childhood idols doing porno films to get by.

Everybody on our e-mail list (around 310 people
across the country) would be at the memorial service.
Celebrities would read jokes that our business had e-mailed
out. Pop stars would tell stories of jokes I told at parties
that were funny and for some reason were never e-mailed
out (bosses vetoed my creative director status). There
would be enlarged photos of a young me laughing while I
was playing with a real-estate loan calculator—maybe the
earliest evidence of my bright future in merging comedy
and technology.

I was jarred back to reality by the chime sound
coming from my laptop, letting me know that I had mail
to read. When I rolled over and checked, I had one e-mail
in my laptop's in box. It was from the Canadian. The note
simply said that he would like to gather the three of us
for a drink after work. Sweet. A free drink. This could be
the very start of the rich part! When we got there, I was
quick at ordering a Coke and he was quick in getting to
the point of the meeting. The stock market had gone
through major adjustments lately (and we're all worth
centimillions?) and unfortunately, after nine months, there
was no longer a budget to keep the business plan up and
running. And so the plug was officially pulled. I went back
to the makeshift office and gathered my personal belong-
ings from on and around my makeshift desk. As I was
walking home to my apartment with a box full of office

items, no job, and rent coming due in a week, it occurred to me that the e-mail that invited me out for a free drink only for me to find all of this out—*this* was the funniest e-mail our little Internet humor venture ever sent out.

RIDDLES FOR A FUNNY WEB SITE
WRITTEN BY A DEPRESSED YOUNG MAN

CLUE: I beg you to embrace me when you are swimming near, but I sting you nearly to death if you dare.

ANSWER: I am despair.

CLUE: Though I lure salmon from the sea, I also tempt you from your clothes when you consider me.

ANSWER: I am the biological drive to reproduce before dying.

CLUE: I am unfamiliar yet somehow the same. I make you see spots and feel pressure or pain.

ANSWER: I am a stranger's hands pressed firmly into your eyes in a moment of struggle.

CLUE: I have held you through the night. Hold me now and I will bite.

ANSWER: I am your ex-girlfriend named Kristin.

CLUE: I seem to answer and cure all of your problems, while at the same time bringing you new ones.

ANSWER: I am a steady job combined with the use and abuse of alcohol.

CLUE: I am the last thing added to the house when it is made, and the first thing you need to get out of the rain.

ANSWER: I am the fifteen thousand dollars' worth of unanticipated landscaping that will prevent you from affording a vacation this winter.

CLUE: Though I may be a bright silver, I am often a force of darkness.

ANSWER: I am a 9mm pistol carried by an angry member of a popular gang.

E-MAIL

June 13, 1999

Dear M,
So my job, and the Internet company it was at, have been gone for ten business days now. Which, in light of the last month or two, seems fine with me. My little dot-com job was starting to feel like being in one of those bubblegum pop boy-bands, and that behind our attempts to woo America's moms in shopping malls with our noon

concerts, we were really falling into the tour bus (van) every afternoon hating each other. Hating decisions made within the band by each other, and hating certain styles of certain members . . . even though we were aware that we needed this chorus of diverse styles to remain appealing. We needed the cute computer geek. We needed the sleepier bad seed turned good. We needed the untraditionally handsome Australian business-genius-boy-man-thing.

Here is the truth: WE RARELY SANG OUR OWN SONGS.

We were busy rallying ourselves to monitor the mundane tasks that ultimately killed us, like creating documents that would outline strategies for getting our work done by people with talent in order to fuel our little show. And so we stood on our little stage day after day in the mall and I secretly steeped in hatred over the fact that the very thing that made us want to try this was now something we didn't even do ourselves. I'm a little bit tired in a way that I can't really put a finger on. After three days by the ocean in Montauk, getting burned by the sun, seven business days later my skin is shedding. Most of it. Maybe even all of it. As if I'll slither from it in my sleep and leave it here. And somebody hiking through my apartment building, seasons later, will find it and guess my size and my stature and my current whereabouts. It's a shedding that makes me think I should not take job interviews. So I sit in my apartment looking out at the city, drinking popular brands of bottled iced-coffee drinks (two left) and eating nutrition bars (four left), convincing myself that when the peeling is done, I will be something new and somehow ready for whatever is next.

QUESTIONS WITH SECRET ANSWERS THAT CUSTOMER SERVICE WILL ASK IN ORDER TO HELP ME REMEMBER MY E-MAIL PASSWORDS

Q: Who is not a pile of laundry or a monster, but is often mistaken for both when you wake suddenly after having dozed off at your place of employment? (First *and* last names here, please.)

Q: If you are drunk and eating sushi, where will you find your squeamish friend and what garment would he most likely be draped in? Hint: It is the same thing you try to fit into usually after having too much to drink.

Q: Never mind that many a weekend was spent and wrecked by trying to get her to laugh or smile or at least forget about her mountain of personal debt and irreparable social miscues: Now that your ex-girlfriend Kristin is gone, what quality of hers do you miss?

Q: What would the man on the bike who rides around on Eighth Street all day lose if it wasn't attached to his handlebars? Hint: It's not a cup holder, and it can pick up CB radio conversations.

Q: You tried to play a drum solo when you spent the night at his house in the seventh grade, it was late, and his sister had some kind of asthma attack. Your late-night outburst on the drum set is still thought to have been the reason the family had to rush her to an emergency room that night, even though there is absolutely *no logical reason* for sound to have anything to do with triggering any kind of reaction, asthmatic or otherwise, in a person's lungs, especially when she was sleeping *downstairs*. He still hasn't really forgiven you for the scare that his sister was put through. Who is the friend I am referring to?

Q: They are bitter, they are not interested in men, they are on the second floor, and they smoke marijuana while watching daytime TV. Who are they and how do they regard you?

Q: Let's say that I bend the rules regarding dating a customer, and I sleep with somebody I meet on the support line after they have forgotten their password—you, for instance. Would I fall in love with you, and if so, what qualities would I most or least admire?

11

Note to Self:

Figure Out Rest of Life

- Walking alone down crowded, hot, noisy Canal
  Street. Filled mostly with lost tourists and
  sturdy-looking Chinese women hawking fake
  designer sunglasses and unlicensed Simpsons
  T-shirts. Carrying everything I had at the office
  in a cardboard box that smells like rotten lettuce.
  Made me think of that scene in *The Jerk* with
  Steve Martin. The one where he's left with the
  wooden paddle with the rubber ball stapled to
  long rubber-band-like string. Also had a chair,
  I think. And a Thermos. Maybe when you see

a crazy person carrying a bunch of crap in an old box and walking on the streets laughing out loud, it's just an everyday person who lost his Internet job and is thinking of *The Jerk* with Steve Martin.

- Sitting in apartment with plastic bag of groceries, and box of desk items and coffee cup from work. Also my laptop. Groceries are mostly nutrition bars—smart move since job is gone—three square meals for three dollars and thirty cents a day . . . plus . . . gets you in shape! Also got two-pound bag of rice. Calming story on back of bag about how the rice was grown by same guy who used to swim in lane five every morning at five-thirty at health club where I worked. Little picture of him on back of bag. First time I've seen him in years. Feels good to see a familiar face three thousand miles from where I started. Also bought coffee and Ginkgo biloba.
- Reading books I brought home from office about salesmanship and negotiating.

Core Competencies

???

Whatever.

- Mass-market paperbacks on sales and CEO biographies are becoming my religion. *WWTGWSDPD: What Would the Guy Who Started Domino's Pizza Do? Dave's Way* is good. About guy who started Wendy's. I am

a Single with everything. The books make me
feel connected to something larger. I see the
so-called coincidences that occur when reading
Herb Cohen's *You Can Negotiate Anything* from
page one while at the same moment starting
Cheap Trick at Budokan on side one, track one:

PAGE 1

BOOK: Your real world is a giant negotiating
table, and like it or not, you're a participant.
RECORD: All right, Tokyo! Are you ready?!

PAGE 15

BOOK: How you handle encounters can determine
not only whether you prosper, but whether you
can enjoy a full, responsible life.
RECORD: Hello there, ladies and gentlemen,
hello there, ladies and gents / Are you ready
to rock? Are you ready or not?

PAGE 17

BOOK: I perceived that there might be a problem.
"I've had a rough day," she murmured.
RECORD: Oooh, baby, feels so good. Don't you
go ruin it tonight, tonight / Been so long, since
I don't know when

PAGE 25

BOOK: Don't act as though your experience repre-
sents universal truths.

RECORD: There is some place, one place in the world/Where I wanna take you, Look out, look out [This one doesn't coincide so much, maybe.]

- <u>Something I haven't thought of until now:</u>
  The only way to figure out what you naturally do, and are naturally good at, is to take some time to do nothing and just see what happens.
    In my case, this is what happens:
    - Sleep
    - Drink coffee
    - Read
    - Eat
    - Write in totally gay-in-the-seventh-grade-sense-of-the-word blank journal
    - Read things I write in gay little journal to small crowds of strangers at open-mic things in bars and cafés
    - Watch TV
    - Eat again
    - Sleep again

Old man in a bar: "When I was younger, I used to wonder what I wanted to do with my life, but I learned it's not what you *want* to do, it's what you *can* do."

- Maybe I can write a book? Freelance-writing ad copy to get by.

Recent Budget Cuts in Eating Habits
JUNE: Hummus platters from the Olive Tree Café on MacDougal Street ($4.50)

JULY: Little tofu squares with a zucchini ($3.50 total) from market on Bleecker Street called Fresh Vegetables Cigarettes Soda

AUGUST: Chicken tacos from California Taqueria in Brooklyn ($1.75)

• Guy at reading/gig last night introduced me to an agent, and I called her. Supposed to send her something called a "proposal." Sent these notes I've been writing since losing my job about six months ago. Used credit card to FedEx it to her Priority Overnight. Life's finally going to change, and it's going to happen by ten o'clock the next business morning. Sweet. Finally. Try a prayer, even though I don't know any:

Thank you, God or Moses or whatever, for bringing a cornucopia horn . . . filled with . . . an agent . . . to my manger . . . of wise lambs . . . With the lights out, it's less dangerous. All is quiet on New Year's Day. Jeremy has spoken. Amen.

• Agent called me at home today around noon!!! After we exchanged pleasant hellos, she asked me why I sent her a bunch of notes.

"Uh, proposal, you mean?"

"Notes. There's some e-mail . . . and some notes that I guess you—"

"Right. I know. A proposal . . . for a book of, uh . . . notebooks that, um, tell a *story*. How long will it take to get an advance on that?"

- Turns out, you can't just send the agent your
  e-mail and notes and get money, although I think
  you can do this if you're a felon, as only months
  later I saw something like this in a men's
  magazine. A guy had killed several people and
  then sent the magazine some letters and the
  magazine put all of the letters together into a
  feature piece. Murder is out of the question
  for me.

Have sent (again) what I think is a book proposal.

- Have gotten several calls, though none are *Jerry
  Maguire* "Show me the money" call. Did get a
  Mrs. Maguire "We need the money" call from
  American Express. Also heard from "Steve" at
  Bank of America MasterCard. It's good to hear
  Steve is well. It's been thirty days since the last
  time he called.

- Book proposal sold! Celebrate by buying three-
  hundred-dollar shirt from a store I used to never
  be able to afford. I charge it on Amex. Will pay
  off in thirty days when book check comes.

- Agent called today and said money doesn't come
  until *after* you sign the contract, and the contract
  will take about three months to get, and *then* will
  get a third of the advance. Okay. But
  still . . . book proposal sold. Need to see if I can
  actually write a book instead of just notes.
  Maybe the only reason we don't do half of the
  things we try to do in life is because we just never
  get around to doing them. No, like, big dramatic

or mystical reason. Just never start or try and so we never finish. SO, TRY TO START.

Trying

Once upon a time Mr. Author looked at the bills piling up on his "writing desk," so Mr. Fancy Shirt decided he would need to be hitting the streets desperately and quickly, looking for work in a very slow economy. And so, Mr. Author Writer found himself, advertising portfolio under arm, interviewing back with the very first marketing agency in Connecticut where he first landed after getting off the plane from Seattle almost six years ago. A temporary freelance position, but a long one. Maybe three months. I reintroduced myself to the creative director and he remembered me and handed me more pictures of skin softener and vodka than I ever thought I would ever see again.

He kind of just paused and looked at me and said, "Hey, we met a *real* long time ago, right? Like six years ago, when you were Mr. Cool Guy from Seattle."

So now each day, for the next few months, I get on the subway at seven-thirty in the morning, and I ride on it all the way up to Grand Central Station. Then at Grand Central Station I get on a train to Connecticut at eight, and then I walk along the side of a small highway in Connecticut at about 9:15, and then I walk through pleasant suburban residential streets at about 9:45, and then finally I walk (a little bit sweaty) into the agency at about ten A.M. During the day I sit in a cubicle and write the kind of stuff that falls out of your Sunday papers or the kind of things that clutter up the dairy aisle of your favorite supermarket. And so I write the copy in colorful newspaper inserts in which I tell all of you that your skin really could be younger-looking and more radiant. I write the copy for the posters and static-cling decals in the dairy aisle of your favorite grocer that remind you that your kids need calcium and vitamin D in their yogurt. It's the only work I turn up, and I know it's considered unglamorous by advertising people, but it pays the same or better on any given day, and I've never understood the elitism within the advertising business. Why is it considered more glamorous to write a TV commercial about a little Hispanic dog who tells you that you should have a particular brand of fast-food burrito for lunch than to write a brochure about a little polar bear who really wants you to have some frozen yogurt for dessert? And things feel different knowing that I have a book to write. Knowing that I've figured out what I do at least for a minute. I write the book in any free minute I have at work. And at the end of each day, I retrace my steps back through the neighborhood, along the small highway, and then onto the train I'm currently writing to you from, which takes me back to the city. Today when I was walking down an endless maze of white picket fences back to the train station, a little boy playing in his front yard runs up to the fence to look at me. I'm leaving his street, getting ready to make a right and walk on the side of the highway for the remaining mile or so to the train stop, and he runs up to the fence, looks at me with eyes that take it all in. I'm wearing a little too much black and looking not quite like a dad. Totally out of place walking past the pleasant suburban houses, I must look like the criminal from a Disney movie to him. Or maybe I'm obviously somehow too defeated to be really dangerous or bad, and that's why he feels comfortable coming up to me, and for the first time in my life I'm feeling like things are working out and I have somehow strangely always been in the right place at the right time . . . even the times that were all wrong. So I'm in this mood that makes me know this kid has been put in my path for a reason as well. Maybe he'll say something so accurate it's chilling, like some kind of fortune-teller, since kids can see the truth and ghosts and UFOs.

Maybe he will say, "Start writing. On the train. Tonight. In that gay little journal you carry around with you. It's what you naturally do, ever since the sixth grade, except this time it will be notes for the book. You'll be like a huge, thirty-three-year-old goony sixth-grader with a book deal writing on some lame-ass commuter train. Now go! Go on!"

Whatever he says, he will deliver the message that all of us have lost the ability to say in our jaded adult lives. Maybe about how our lives finally change but only when it is right for our lives to change. That we are not in control of this thing. I look back at him just before making my right turn onto the highway for the last part of my walk to the train. It feels like slow motion as he sizes me up that one last time. He opens his mouth and the words come out:

"Hey, mister. Why don't you have a car?"

Oh, man.

The End

ACKNOWLEDGMENTS

The Author Wishes to Thank:

William Russell Kennedy and Lori Ann
Kennedy, Trish Kennedy Dwairi and
Raed Dwairi.

Maria Lilja. Jim Levine, Arielle Eckstut,
and everybody at Levine-Greenberg
Communications. Doug Pepper, Steve Ross,
Jason Gordon, Juleyka Lantigua, and
everyone at Crown. Timothy McSweeney's
Internet Tendency. George Dawes Greene,
Lea Thau, Jenifer Hixson, Catherine Burns,
and Stories At The Moth. Joey Xanders,
Joshua Wolf Shenk, Jerry Stahl, John Murphy,
Paul Maliszewski, Neal Pollack, Jonathan
Ames, Sarah Vowell, Paul Tough, Scott
Dikkers, Whitney Pastorek, Jim Sharp,
John Keister, Cam Hopkins, Sheri Howell,
Loren Victory, Andrew Hultkrans, Deborah

Copaken Kogan, Amy Maguire, Ben Whitten, Lisa Ashcraft, Vicky Germaise, Sara Shenasky. Jim Smith, Martha Ritchie, and Abbie Moriarity of Paradise High School. Scott Salfen and Tom Bassani of 1991 USFS Mendocino OC27.

ABOUT THE AUTHOR

Dan Kennedy lives in New York.